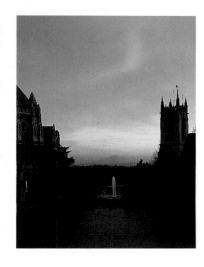

The Fountain & the Mountain

THE UNIVERSITY OF WASHINGTON CAMPUS 1895–1995

Text by
Norman J. Johnston

Foreword by
Brewster C. Denny

Documentary Book Publishers Corporation
Woodinville, Washington

and

University of Washington
Seattle, Washington

Dedicated to the memory of

Gordon B. Varey
1931–1994

*Dean of the University of Washington College
of Architecture and Urban Planning, 1982–1992
Chair of the University of Washington
Architectural Commission, 1982–1994*

The Fountain & the Mountain
The University of Washington Campus 1895–1995
Copyright © 1995 Documentary Book Publishers Corporation and The University
of Washington

For information, write Documentary Book Publishers Corporation, P.O. Box 1951,
Woodinville, Washington 98072-1951.

Author: Norman J. Johnston
Editors: Robert Spector, Joyce Brewster
Copy Editor: Judy Gouldthorpe, with assistance from Jessica Eber
Cover and book design: Marquand Books, Inc.
Publisher: Barry Provorse
Printed in Hong Kong

PAGE 1: Spring, University of Washington. *Photo: Loyd Heath*
PAGE 2: University of Washington seal. *Photo: Stewart Hopkins*

Library of Congress Catalog Card Number: 95-69435
Johnston, Norman J.
The Fountain & the Mountain
The University of Washington Campus 1895–1995
ISBN 0-935503-15-3
1. History
2. Architecture
3. University of Washington
4. Seattle

Contents

7   Acknowledgments

10   Foreword

13   **PART ONE**   The Evolution of the Present Campus

15   Chapter One   Founding of the University

27   Chapter Two   The Alaska-Yukon-Pacific Exposition

37   Chapter Three   Suzzallo's "University of a Thousand Years"

47   Chapter Four   The Postwar Campus Evolution and Charles E. Odegaard

63   Chapter Five   William P. Gerberding and the Politics of Growth

72   **PART TWO**   Campus Design, Architecture, and Landscape

75   Chapter Six   North Campus

95   Chapter Seven   Central Campus

151   Chapter Eight   South Campus

168   Suggested Reading

169   Index

Acknowledgments

MY FIRST MEMORIES OF THE UNIVERSITY OF WASHINGTON, SOME SEVENTY
years ago, were environmental: a row of salmon-pink geraniums topping the wall of
the northwest campus that parallels Fifteenth Avenue Northeast. That began a love
affair with this campus that is still with me. My informal collection of materials of
more recent years related to campus history was thus put to good use when the University of Washington invited me to write this book.

In doing so, I have been given encouragement and assistance by others, who deserve mention here: Library Specialist Gary Lundell and the resources of the University Library's Manuscript and Archives Division; the former University Architect
Ed Duthweiler and Capital Projects Director Connie Miller; Development Director
Lyn Firkins, my colleague in the College of Architecture and Urban Planning; Associate Vice President for University Relations Norm Arkans; University associates whom I interviewed and who added their reflections on their role in campus
development, notably Charles Odegaard, Fred Mann, and the late Ernie Conrad;
Brewster Denny, who contributed valuable correspondence and suggestions; Joyce
Brewster, who lent editorial assistance; and Barry Provorse, the book's enthusiastic
publisher, to whom much of the credit goes for the handsome production this book
has become.

But my richest resource has been the physical evidence of the campus itself: its
buildings, its vistas, and its landscape are collective testimony to the commitment
and care it has over the years received from those responsible for its nurturing and
support. What better observance of the one-hundredth anniversary of the University's move to this wonderful site than to appreciate the magnificent campus
around us as we celebrate this historic event.

Norman J. Johnston
Professor Emeritus of Architecture,
Landscape Architecture, and Urban Design and Planning
College of Architecture & Urban Planning
University of Washington

LEFT: Suzzallo Library windows, Smith Wing
Photo: Jeff Zaruba
ABOVE: Norman J. Johnston
Photo: Stewart Hopkins
OVERLEAF: Liberal Arts Quadrangle
Photo: Loyd Heath

Foreword

AS WE CELEBRATE THE FIRST HUNDRED YEARS OF THE PRESENT UNIVERSITY of Washington campus, it is fitting that we have Norman Johnston's fine account of the first century of this campus. This is a distinguished book—the work of a professional who knows his trade, and a proud son and professor of a fine institution.

As a descendant of University and Seattle founders Arthur and Mary Denny, I often visit grade-school classes studying Seattle history. A fourth-grader once asked me, "How long did it take them to build the University of Washington?" My answer was, "I don't know—they aren't done yet." Today's campus is but a piece of a long story, not yet all told.

Ten years after settlers landed at Alki (pronounced Al-key)—when the town had only two hundred people, when it was totally remote from the rest of the world and was neither the largest nor the most promising village in the wilderness, before it had a primary or secondary school building, well before it had qualified university students—the University and its land represented an audacious bet on the future by sturdy pioneers, and a declaration of Jeffersonian faith in the value of learning by citizens in charge of a free country.

Public policy had already blazed the trail to education. Beginning with Thomas Jefferson and the Northwest Ordinance, new lands in every territory were set aside for education. Like the history of the United States, the history of its universities is the history of land. And when the University of Washington's first beautiful knoll in the woods—that initial private gift of land we now call the Metropolitan Tract—became too small an urban place for a campus, pioneering a new piece of land for education again became a down payment on the state's future.

It is that second campus that we celebrate this year and honor with this splendid work. We note that the first increment of the present campus was Mr. Jefferson's school land, and that significant additions to the land of the present campus were bought with income from the Metropolitan Tract. A substantial percentage of the present value of the University lands and buildings comes from income from the federal lands and the Tract, both great gifts secured by the University's founders. As the late Edward E. Carlson said, "This great endowment and the institution it supports will have to last for a long time, maybe forever."

Starting with land, then, this story is about buildings and people as well. The names on today's campus structures honor many who played major roles in building this university. Bagley, Denny, Meany, Miller, Gould, Suzzallo, Odegaard come first to mind—names that exemplify the strong personal leadership essential to building a physical campus environment. This theme continues in the sixteen-year presidency of William P. Gerberding, which ends this centennial year. As trustee of

ABOVE: Brewster C. Denny
Photo: Stewart Hopkins

10

this "princely endowment in lands"—the phrase is from Charles Gates's *The First Century at the University of Washington*—President Gerberding has secured the most substantial state funding for capital construction in the University's history, and has guided construction of an architecturally brilliant and environmentally sensitive group of new buildings. He also has led the most successful raising of private donations since that first great gift of land 134 years ago that started it all.

Prominent in this story is the architectural history itself: the aesthetics of the buildings; how they became what they are; how landscaping and environmentally sensitive siting, beginning in Charles Odegaard's time, became a real commitment to preserving the character of the place just as space constraints began to force a more urban quality on a pastoral campus of great beauty. Walk in spring in the quad among the blossoms, and thank Odegaard for that, as well as for the surge of intellectual quality that marked his years. Look at the vital new buildings, from the Allen Library to the new science buildings, that still preserve the sylvan feel of the place, and thank William Gerberding and Tallman Trask.

Public universities have a special place in the history of the world. The other democracies have their Oxford, Cambridge, Heidelberg, Leiden, Oslo, and Sorbonne, and America has its Harvard, MIT, Yale, Princeton, and Stanford. But the great American state universities, California, Michigan, Wisconsin, Illinois, North Carolina, Washington, and all the others across the country, are a special breed—started with public land and supported by the states. More important, they account for the fact that a far larger percentage of our citizens, particularly those of limited means and minority and immigrant roots, have received high-quality education in the arts and sciences and professions than any other place in the world. This story is about that as well. At the margin, as economists would say, this educational edge has been critical and, if maintained against present severe jeopardy, will be critical in the future to Americans' place in the world.

Cathedrals and universities, along with music, literature, and art, may be humankind's most permanent physical expressions of the loftiest aspirations of the human spirit—learning and compassion and respect for the worth of man and nature. Norman Johnston has captured the events and the spirit of a remarkable story, one that began on the edge of a frontier with the idea that a university building, even before there were college-level students to study there, was a pledge to a bright future. As the Alma Mater says, "In honor thy towers stand."

Brewster C. Denny
Professor Emeritus and Dean Emeritus of Public Affairs
University of Washington

The Evolution of the Present Campus

WELCOME TO WASHINGTON, THE UNIVERSITY OF A THOUSAND YEARS, AND

to a campus in which nature, time, design, and luck have produced one of the nation's finest examples of how a designed environment can realize its full potential. Today, the campus stands as a dynamic work of art for students, faculty, visitors, and all of the people of the state of Washington.

In a college community, environment matters. Sixty percent of college-bound students cited the environmental quality of the campus as *the most important factor* in determining the college of their choice, according to a recent study for the Carnegie Foundation. Environment also plays an important role in the career decisions of faculty and staff.

Thus, the campus becomes a primary asset in the University's pursuit of the brightest and the best. In the Thomas A. Gaines 1991 analysis of the environmental quality of the nation's campuses—based on their open spaces, architectural quality, landscape, and overall appeal—the University of Washington was given a score of eighteen out of a possible twenty. When the nation's top university architects met on our campus in 1994, one delegate was quoted as saying that he "truly believe[d] this is the best planned, best sited, most beautifully and sensitively designed and built campus in the world."

How did we get that way? This book has been published both to explore that question and to celebrate the results.

Part One is a historical overview of the basics that explains the evolutionary development of the campus environment, with focus on some of the key personalities, goals, and circumstances that shaped its two-dimensional plan on the land.

Part Two offers something of the circumstances and history of the various campus elements—natural and built—that give three-dimensional form to the campus plan, and explores the role those elements play in its drama. The campus sectors are each composed of the same panoply of elements—forms, spaces, axes, patterns, buildings, and landscapes—that work together (calculatedly or inadvertently) toward determining what the sector has come to be. But there the similarities substantially end; each sector is unique, shaped by its site, its function, and the versatility with which the designers interpreted it.

The publication of this book is timely, for in 1995 the University honors the history of its move one hundred years ago from downtown to this campus. The book also commemorates the sixteen years of William P. Gerberding's tenure as twenty-seventh president of the University. In the Gerberding era, 1979 to 1995, some twenty-eight major architectural projects were either completed or well on their way to completion. Dr. Gerberding's record of achievement is, in part, revealed in what we see around us as we move from building to building, quadrangle to quadrangle, landscaped lawn to wooded grove. Each of these elements plays a role in the complex of space and form, beauty and splendor that is today's University of Washington campus.

LEFT: Physics/Astronomy Building
Photo: NBBJ/Timothy Hursley
ABOVE: Sundial
Photo: Stewart Hopkins

CHAPTER ONE

Founding of the University

FROM ITS BEGINNINGS, THE UNIVERSITY WAS INSPIRED BY THE AUDACIOUS
goals of Washington Territorial pioneers. Money was no object because they had
none. Nevertheless, their dreams were abetted by congressional legislation that in
1854 had reserved forty-six thousand timbered acres specifically for support of a university. The following year, the territorial legislature provided that a university be established in the two-year-old village of Seattle, with a branch campus in the more
populous Lewis County, both "on the same footing with respect to funds and all
other matters." But matters, both political and patronage, happily intervened to
thwart those clumsy potentials.

Now the initiative passed to Seattle, a "drab and unattractive" village, where two
of its two hundred souls realized the potential offered by locating the university in
their midst. One was an original settler, Arthur A. Denny, the other was the Reverend Daniel Bagley, a classically trained Methodist and native New Yorker who in
1860 brought new inspiration to these efforts. Bagley worked with Denny and Joseph Foster, both of whom had been elected to represent King County in the 1861
territorial legislature.

In that colorful era of unabashed frontier promotion, a typical ploy of specula-
tors in nascent communities was to include—in the bright visions of their gridded
development plans—at least one desirable public institution, which would help
enhance the town's future prospects as well as boost its attractions for potential
investors. Toward getting a university for Seattle, Denny assembled a coalition of
legislators, each with his own special interest and a desire to swap favors. Port
Townsend's representative sought a government land office for his town; Vancouver's representative wanted his southwestern Washington town designated as
the territorial capital; and Walla Walla's legislator lobbied for a penitentiary. Denny
promised his support if they would back his project.

It worked. The 1861 legislature sited the university in Seattle and established a
University Land Commission, whose first appointees included Seattle residents
Edmund Carr, John Webster, and the Reverend Mr. Bagley, who was also named its
president.

The legislature also stipulated that no fewer than ten acres had to be donated for
the campus. Arthur Denny, in turn, donated Denny's Knoll, an eight-and-a-half-acre
site on his prime forested claim overlooking Elliott Bay. To reach the ten-acre minimum, he helped secure a one-and-a-half-acre piece of adjoining land held by Charles
and Mary Terry and Edward Lander.

With the zeal of his religious calling and the skill of a horse trader, Bagley took
charge. Soon to be known as "the man who stole the University for the City of
Seattle," he directed land sales and oversaw the clearing of the tract. To get the work
done, Bagley offered home sites in exchange for carpentry skills, persuaded some
individuals to work at bargain rates, and convinced others to volunteer their time

LEFT: Denny Hall, originally called the
Administration Building, was the University's
first building on its new campus.
*Photo: University of Washington, News and
Information*
TOP: Arthur Denny
*Photo: University of Washington Libraries,
Special Collections and Preservation Division*
ABOVE: The Reverend Daniel Bagley
*Photo: University of Washington Libraries,
Special Collections and Preservation Division*

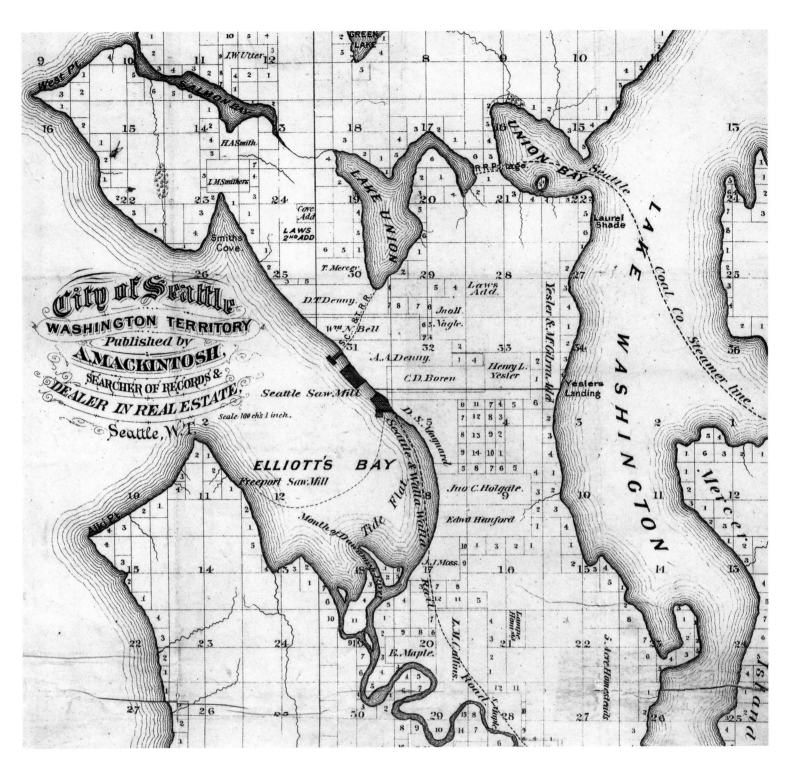

TOP: 1870s Seattle claims map
*Photo: University of Washington Libraries,
Special Collections and Preservation Division*
ABOVE: Seattle, 1860s
Photo: MOHAI, Seattle Historical Society Collection

for the betterment of the community. Bagley also traded acreage to the Port Madison Mill for white pine lumber that would be used to erect the University's first buildings. Amid flag-waving ceremonies, the cornerstone was laid on May 20, 1861.

Seattle pioneer John Pike (for whom Seattle's Pike Street is named) designed the first building, a stately two-storied structure that featured an elegantly sculptured Ionic-columned portico, a balustered roofline, and a belfry (the bell brought round the Horn). From its heights, facing south, the building's white presence dominated for years the skyline above the modest framed structures that sprinkled Seattle's logged-off slopes and shoreline below.

Also built on the new campus were a two-story frame house for University President Asa Shinn Mercer and a "plain box" dormitory for boys. The girls lived in Mercer's house, under the supervision of his wife. (The University could board no more than thirty students.) When these first buildings were completed, the campus was enclosed with a white picket fence. In all, the project cost $30,400.69, paid for by an appropriation from the legislature.

September 16, 1861, marked the opening of the Territorial University of Wash-

ington, the first public institution of higher learning on the West Coast. Classes began officially on November 4, with Mercer as the only instructor. (The first university-level degree would not be granted until 1876.)

The University's early years were marked by economic and academic uncertainties, including limited support from the territorial legislature, several temporary closures, deteriorating physical facilities, an inadequate supply of students prepared for university-level work (a preparatory program—in common English, history, algebra, and physiology—was maintained intermittently to fill that void), and frequent turnover of presidents (six in fifteen years). Items in the minutes of the Board of Regents, which was charged with governing the University, reflect the rigors of sustaining a poor pioneer institution: repair of the white picket fence along Union Street, expense not to exceed $15; an appropriation of $3.20 for snow removal from campus walks; $16 for repair of the campus pump; and a ruling that no cows or other livestock be allowed on the campus.

The Evolution of the Present Campus

By the end of the 1880s, the University had slowly begun to prosper along with the city of Seattle, whose population had reached more than 40,000, and the territory, which was home to more than 350,000. The University's enrollment, approaching three hundred, was becoming a burden on the campus, while the city's tavern district, traditionally along Skid Road, had begun to encroach on Denny's Knoll. Seeing little room for growth, University boosters began talk of a new campus.

Washington's elevation to statehood in 1889 helped translate that talk into action. The territorial legislature had provided the University with only marginal financial and moral support, but the new state legislature was more generous, not only with its purse but also with its recognition of the University's potential and the degree to which its current circumstances impeded its development.

A special legislative committee examined those circumstances and agreed with the Board of Regents that there was need for change. According to its 1889 report, "The grounds of the university in the city of Seattle are in a pitiably neglected and forlorn condition, and have been so for years. An old ramshackle fence surrounds them, and often in places knocked or blown down, cows invade and trespass."

ABOVE LEFT: The University (to the right of the church) as it appeared on the Seattle skyline during the 1870s
Photo: MOHAI, Seattle Historical Society Collection
ABOVE RIGHT: University of Washington, 1870s
Photo: University of Washington Libraries, Special Collections and Preservation Division

This was followed in the 1890 report by an explicit call for action: "Ampler grounds are essential to the prosperity and well-being of the university, and grounds more remote from the center of a rapidly growing and expanding city. . . [the campus is] best removed from the excitements and temptations incident to city life and its environments."

The report concluded by asking for legislative authority to sell the old campus and find another campus more suitable in both location and area. The legislature granted that authority—including selection of a new site of at least forty acres "conveniently near the city"—to a separate board of University Land and Building Commissioners, since the regents were thought to be already busy enough. From that legislative action flowed the events that led to the University's present site.

The new University Land and Building Commission, established by the legislature in 1891, included among its members Elisha P. Ferry (first governor of Washington State); Seattle businessman and University regent James R. Hayden; John Arthur, a Seattle attorney with considerable knowledge of University properties; John McReavey, a prominent Democrat; and Charles F. Leavenworth of Olympia. The legislature directed the new commissioners to clarify the old land grant, remedy defects in the deeds to the Denny tract so that the old University grounds could be sold, acquire new grounds, and construct suitable buildings on the new site.

Unfortunately, since falling lumber prices had brought down the state's economy, there was little support for investing in the University's future. But that failed to deter a journalist and promoter named Edmond S. Meany. In the history of the University and its campuses, the contributions of the six-foot-six-inch Meany, an 1885 graduate of the University, rank along with those of Daniel Bagley and Arthur Denny. In 1891, Meany was elected to the state legislature; part of his platform was advancing the University's interests. He became chairman of the university committee in the lower house and, later, chairman of the legislative joint committee that was created to find, acquire, and guide a new campus.

The legislature's specifications for the new site called for one located within six miles of its present site for exclusive university use and increased its size to a minimum of one hundred acres. Several potential sites were considered that met those requirements: Jefferson Park, Fort Lawton, and Interlaken (the present-day site). The latter had already attracted the interest of University president Thomas M. Gatch, who so informed Meany. Although Meany agreed with Gatch, he thought it politic

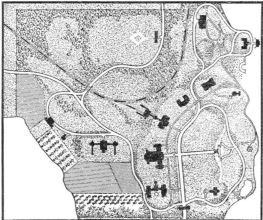

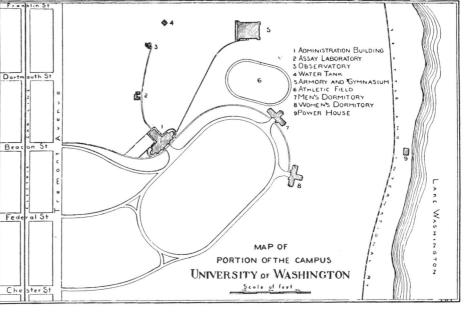

TOP: Edmond Meany
Photo: University of Washington Libraries, Special Collections and Preservation Division
ABOVE LEFT: 1891 Boone Plan for the University's campus
Photo: University of Washington Libraries, Special Collections and Preservation Division
ABOVE RIGHT: The Oval Plan, also known as the Fuller Plan, 1898
Photo: University of Washington Libraries, Special Collections and Preservation Division

to let his legislative colleagues draw their own conclusions by bringing them to Seattle for on-site viewing. The legislators later agreed on the Interlaken site, but wanted only the lower 160 acres of the 580-acre tract. Rather than pressing the issue, Meany, who wanted it all, bided his time. In the meantime, the University's downtown campus was appraised at $250,000, but the poor city economy meant little interest and no buyers for the site. Title to the old campus was cleared, however, and the University Land and Building Commission began planning the new campus.

With unusual initiative, the commissioners hired a local architect, William E. Boone, to develop a comprehensive plan for the site. After making inquiries to other universities in this country and abroad, and visiting principal American universities, Boone presented the commissioners with an ambitious plan that included a cluster of five major academic buildings, romantically sited along undulating paths and roads.

On August 20, 1891, the commissioners accepted the Boone plan. Soon after, surveying and clearing of the site began, and work progressed until the construction bids were opened on September 24, 1891. Ranging from $470,000 to more than $650,000, all bids were rejected because they far exceeded available funds. Nor had a buyer been found for the downtown campus.

The University Land and Building Commission considered acting as its own contractor. But the campus project was faced with an unfavorable court decision on the legality of its funding plan and with growing public opposition, including that of Meany, who thought it too extravagant. Meanwhile, Meany's House Bill #470, which was passed on the last day of the 1893 legislative session and signed by Governor McGraw on March 3, 1894, this time authorized purchase of the full Interlaken site (section 16, township 25, north of range 4 east) for $28,313.75. The purchase was backed further by a $150,000 appropriation for construction; Meany's patience had been rewarded. In addition, the legislature abolished the Land and Building Commission and authorized instead a University regents subcommittee responsible for campus development.

The Board of Regents turned quickly to its new tasks. According to the minutes of its meeting of December 13, 1893, the board authorized the removal of some large timber and dead logs (but preserving smaller trees), at the urging of Meany recommended the services of Chicago landscape architect Henry H. Hindshaw for laying out the grounds, and approved a $50 payment to E. O. Schwager for the first building's site planning.

The regents announced a competition for the design of the building, then known as the Administration Building, and on March 14, 1894, awarded the commission to Charles W. Saunders. Construction began following acceptance of a low bid of $112,000. The cornerstone was laid on July 4, 1894, before a civic-minded crowd of nearly one thousand. Later renamed Denny Hall, this would be the first building on the new campus.

The 1894 annual report of the Board of Regents records the progress of events: the hiring of an engineer to make a topographic map of the site and the clearing of about eighty acres of "the highest part of the entire tract forming a fine, undulating plateau . . . selected for building sites and campus [from which] are obtained the most excellent views." The report identifies them: Lake Washington, the Cascades, Lake Union, Puget Sound, and the Olympics—but *no mention of Mount Rainier!* The report continued:

> The balance of the grounds are being mapped out with a view to retain the natural beauty of the spot. Great care is being used to preserve the most desirable trees and shrubbery, because we realize that here we have an opportunity for establishing one of the most important scientific arboretums and botanical gardens of the U.S.

Meany had made much of this site potential in support of acquiring the full tract and enlisted lumber interests at the legislature toward that end. The regents hired Henry Hindshaw, which suggests that they were fully aware of the uniqueness of the University site—planning reminiscent of the earlier Boone efforts.

But in practice this seems not to have been the case. The story (possibly apocryphal) has it that the Administration Building site was chosen by regent David Kellogg, who, after a day viewing the disheveled scene, wearily drove his umbrella into a rotten log and declared that to be the spot. And there it was built, occupied in 1895 and soon followed by other structures: the Observatory (1895), a drill hall, gymnasium, and dressing rooms. Shortly thereafter came two dormitories, Lewis and Clark halls (1899), rather arbitrarily placed, perhaps to accommodate their view potentials overlooking Lake Washington and the distant Cascades.

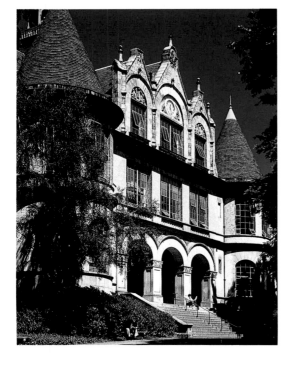

Denny Hall
Photo: Loyd Heath

By the late 1890s, however, the regents were searching for some rationale for locating future buildings and turned to A. H. Fuller, a professor in the Engineering College, to prepare one. The 1898 result became known as the Oval Plan. Extravagant in its use of space, it still incorporated only the upper portion of the tract. Although of uninspired design, the plan did draw the existing buildings into coordinated relationships and establish locations for future ones. Science (now Parrington) Hall (1902) and a power plant were located to conform to it.

Possibly it was the limitations of the Oval Plan that inspired the Board of Regents in August 1903 to approach the Olmsted Brothers, of Brookline, Massachusetts, the major landscape architects of the day, about developing a general campus plan. Impressed by the Olmsteds' recently submitted Seattle Park Plan, the board asked them for a campus plan "in harmony with proposed park system of Seattle . . . [suitable] for many years to come."

In a letter to Colonel Alden Blethen (at the time the board's president), the Olmsteds offered to do a campus plan for $1,000 plus charges for assistants and expenses, and that November the board agreed to those terms. John C. Olmsted visited Seattle and the campus and eventually created the University's 1904 Plan. Unlike the designer of the Oval Plan, Olmsted took into account the full expanse of the site, with its adjoining Fifteenth Avenue to the west, Forty-fifth Street to the north, and the loop of the railroad alignment enclosing the site east- and southward. The firm upheld the basics of the Oval Plan, with its northeasterly alignment and inflated spatial generosity, and titled it Arts Quadrangle, its form reinforced by a complete perimeter of future buildings. To the south was to be a rigidly orthogonal Science Quadrangle and to the west paralleling Fifteenth Avenue, a regimented row of unlikely and disparate neighbors, including the library, gymnasium, president's house, the infirmary, the YMCA, and fraternity row.

BELOW: Clark Hall, 1900
Photo: University of Washington Libraries, Special Collections and Preservation Division
BOTTOM: Olmsted Plan, 1904
Photo: University of Washington Libraries, Special Collections and Preservation Division

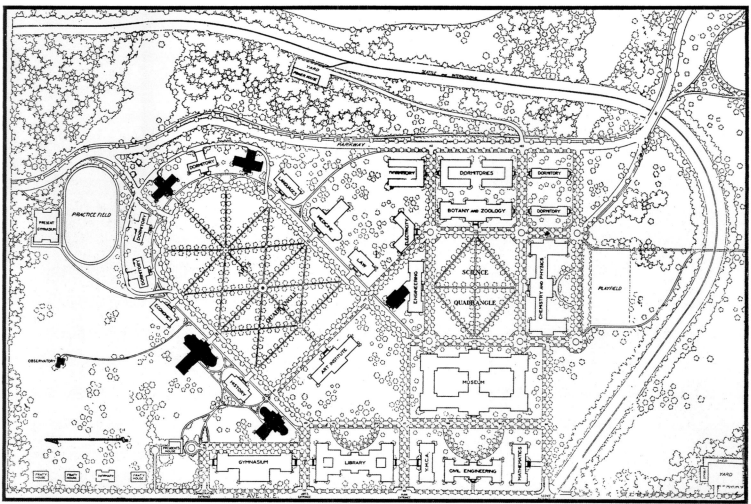

But the plan was essentially self-enclosed, turning inward to the potentials within its own perimeter, neglecting the distant vistas noted by the regents in their 1894 report and, like them, entirely ignoring Mount Rainier. Had the 1904 Plan been realized, the University's campus would no doubt have been satisfactory enough but surely not much more. Fortunately, there came a stroke of luck that saved the campus from that fate and bestowed upon it the design ideas that still inspire us today.

Exposition, Seattle, Wash.

...om the U. S. Government Bldg.

...ka-... ...Pacific Exposition
...ttle, Wi... 1909.

Official Post Card.

X89 A corner of the Forestry Building.

Official Post Card.

X92 Ranier Vista and Music Pavilion.

CHAPTER TWO

The Alaska-Yukon-Pacific Exposition

SEATTLE BUSINESS INTERESTS IN 1906 WERE PLANNING FOR A WORLD'S FAIR, the Alaska-Yukon-Pacific Exposition (AYPE), and had asked the regents to allow it to be placed on the undeveloped lower two-thirds of the campus. Herbert T. Condon, who was business comptroller at the time of the AYPE and would later become one of the younger of the University's grand old men, answered by letter an inquiry in 1932 about that experience:

> In 1907 [*sic*] the Washington State legislature considered the application from the commissioners of the exposition for use of the University campus. At that time of course (pre-Volstead [Prohibition] days) we had a three mile dry zone about the campus. One of the arguments in favor of the campus was that it would be much easier to eliminate liquor traffic in and about the exposition grounds.
>
> . . . the principal inducement the University authorities had, to comply with the suggestion of the joint use of the campus, was the prospect of reducing this wild forest to a finished campus. The legislature gave us our choice of taking a $400,000 building appropriation without any connection with the exposition, or $600,000 and give the exposition temporary use of the buildings that we could build with this amount of money.

Alaska-Yukon-Pacific Exposition
postcards
*Postcards: Documentary Book
Publishers, archive*

But what Condon failed to acknowledge and what was to be a far greater inheritance from the months of the exposition was the *quality* of the campus plan that had been designed for it, which still lay on the land after most of the temporary buildings had been removed.

For the exposition plan, John Olmsted (his firm under contract this time to the AYPE organizers) returned to Seattle, and once again studied the campus environment. Perhaps the day was clear, the sun shone, and Mount Rainier was out in full glory. Because this time, breaking out of the self-contained and inward-looking 1904 campus plan, he recognized the potential for design drama offered by the distant mountain and made it the central theme of his plan and the target of the Rainier Vista axis. But the mountain's capture was elusive (as residents of Seattle will appreciate). In a December 1906 letter to Olmsted, exposition engineer George F. Cotterill wrote that, after many days, his field crew finally had an opportunity to check the trial line toward Mount Rainier, and noted that it required a correction of one-third of a degree to center the mountain peak. "From all points north of the railway, it [Mount Rainier] will loom up magnificently with nothing obstructing," he concluded. That, plus lesser radials toward Lake Washington, the Cascades, Portage Bay, and circumferential routes, provided the exposition with a plan that fully abandoned the 1904 rigidities, one whose versatility realized a full partnership with its environment.

AYPE, 1909
Photo: MOHAI, Seattle Historical Society Collection

When the exposition closed in 1909, the gently southward-sloping campus grounds reverted to the University. Years later Herbert Condon acknowledged the value of the AYPE legacy.

> The greatest assets we realized were: first, the magnificent paved street system and improved transportation lines out from the center of the city . . . and secondly, the clearing of the timber. As far as the buildings were concerned, the only buildings we really considered as assets rather than liabilities were the five permanent brick structures built from the $600,000 . . .

The Regents Plan

The next question was how to meld the grandeur of the former exposition grounds with the uncertain planning of upper campus. The Board of Regents, no doubt pre-occupied with post-exposition adjustments, took a leisurely pace in arriving at any decisions. But in March 1911, the board received a report from President Thomas Kane recommending the hiring of the Olmsted firm to devise "a plan for improvement of the grounds, particularly with a view to future buildings on a symmetrical plan." All of this work was to be performed "with a view to the ultimate plans of the grounds," as best they could determine the "ultimate plans" at that time. In the meantime, Kane recommended, work should continue on the grounds, with "leveling up, surfacing and seeding of the various building sites, the setting out of shrubbery and caring for the lawns, and the clearing and cleaning of the grounds generally."

The regents agreed to follow Kane's recommendation and contact the Olmsted Brothers. The Olmsteds' April 1911 terms appear identical to those of 1903: a preliminary plan for general layout of the grounds for $1,000 plus travel expenses and drafting assistants, with John Olmsted again representing the firm. At its April 25 meeting, the board accepted those terms for the firm's "draft and preliminary plan for laying out of the University grounds which shall show the proposed location of such buildings as we are able to anticipate now and the location of all walks, drives, and athletic fields."

But the resulting Olmsted Brothers Plan of 1914 proved to be a disappointment to its University clients. A joint committee of regents and faculty had been appointed to review campus plans, and in November the group submitted its preliminary report with some major recommendations: accept the quadrangle as a design principle but restudy its Liberal Arts portion; plan for a future main entrance from the north to be aligned with a main axis running north and south from Geyser Basin (today's Frosh Pond); plan for another main entrance from the south aligned with Twenty-third Avenue; subordinate the Fortieth Street entrance in favor of the new north and south entrances; accept collegiate Gothic as the architectural design standard for the campus; establish the University library as the central architectural feature of the grounds; employ an architect to revise the 1914 Plan; and accept the general planning principle "that in the outer fringe of the University the natural plan of landscaping should be retained and in the inner university the formal method." All of these represented significant modification of what the Olmsted firm had offered.

Although the joint committee's report makes no specific mention of it, the Olmsted plan's suggestions for the northwest corner of the campus, with its curvilinear streets and irregularly undulating blocks, were incongruously informal and romantic for uniting with a lower campus whose planning was still dominated by the dramatic classical monumentality and formality of its exposition days. Reexamination was surely called for, and toward that end the joint committee at its meeting in December recommended to the president "that Mr. [Carl F.] Gould be employed to study the present drawings for the general layout of the University grounds, for a period of 6 weeks at a cost not to exceed $300.00." The firm of Bebb and Gould, with Gould as the principal in its work with the University, was duly hired to pursue the contract. Thus, the Olmsted Brothers were dismissed from their long association with the campus, replaced by Gould, who was to have a profound influence on the University in his role as architect, planner, and arbiter of its design future.

Post-AYPE campus
Photo: MOHAI, Seattle Historical Society Collection

Carl F. Gould

Carl F. Gould, a partner in the prominent Seattle architectural firm of Bebb and Gould, was a well-established figure in the community both professionally and socially. The Harvard-educated Gould was already known on campus from his central role in the 1914 founding of a University degree program in architecture. Gould had been appointed lecturer in architecture and charged with developing the new department. The design approach of his European-based Beaux Arts training ideally suited him for translating the City Beautiful monumentality of the AYPE environment into plans compatible with the circumstances of the upper campus and the recommendations of the joint committee.

The impact of his talents is to be seen in the "Revised General Plan of the University of Washington," commonly known as the Regents Plan, the product of a six-month effort by his firm that was accepted by the Board of Regents on May 19, 1915. In the coordinated design symmetry and classical formality of the plan's upper campus extension there is a clear reaffirmation of the spirit found originally in the plan developed for the exposition but awkwardly extended or abandoned in the Olmsteds' 1914 upper campus proposals.

Building on the Olmsteds' earlier quadrangle concept, Gould was far more successful in unifying the planning dynamics of lower and upper campus. In that context, Science Quadrangle was grouped around the exposition's Geyser Basin (Frosh Pond), while upper campus retained the Oval Plan's axial orientation, though with a much more compressed and humanely scaled Liberal Arts Quadrangle.

Uniting the two quadrangles were separate axes whose terminals met in a great central quadrangle (now Central Plaza) before the projected main library, an ensemble of space and form that would, as Gould later wrote, "serve equally the administrative as well as the intellectual needs of the entire institution," celebrating in spatial terms those key roles that unite the arts with the sciences. Thus, the Regents

TOP: University of Washington campus, 1914
Photo: University of Washington Libraries, Special
Collections and Preservation Division
ABOVE: Carl F. Gould
Photo: University of Washington Libraries, Special
Collections and Preservation Division

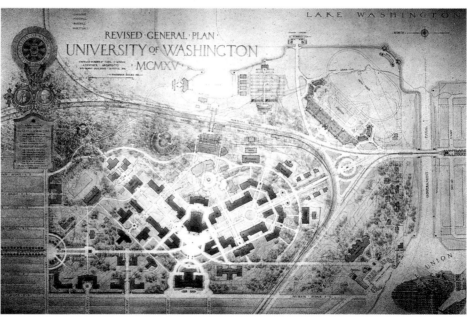

Plan instituted principles for a campus design framework based on a hierarchy of axes, spaces, and forms that continues to underlie the planning of the campus today.

Much of the Regents Plan's Beaux Arts monumentality was almost inevitably expressed in architectural designs based on classical, especially Roman, forms (e.g., the 1893 Chicago World's Fair or the AYPE). No doubt influenced by Gould, the plan chose another model: the joint committee included a recommendation that collegiate Gothic be the architectural form for future campus construction. As was explained in a later presidential document, probably one of President Suzzallo's,

We made a careful study of our climatic and other working conditions at our campus. Because our climate is gray, we adopted a style of

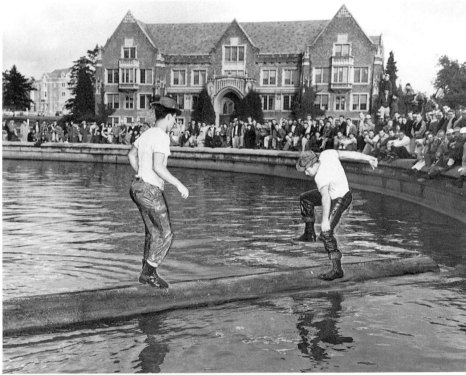

architecture which provided a maximum of light so as to cut down the overhead of artificial lighting. Because our climate is monotonous gray, we put all our buildings in color. Because the color of our climate is suggestively cool, we have broken the effect through the use of warm colors, precisely as the monotony of the white and hot light in the Mediterranean is broken by cool colors.

Emphasis was instead placed on architecture that welcomed planning informality, large window areas, irregular plans and skylines, and a color palette of rich and warm tones of brown, blue, rose, and green. Gould was aware that the collegiate-Gothic choice embraced those qualities and worked well with contemporary structural technology, while also encouraging irregularity of plan and form. This was in contrast to the demands of symmetry, balance, and uniform rooflines so much favored by the classical tradition. On an emotional level, the associations of the Gothic

18 61

Home Economics Building

University of Washington

19 16

Bebb and Gould drawing for the Home Economics Building (now Raitt Hall)

Photo: The Seattle Times, *photo archive*

style, with its overtones of the English universities of Oxford and Cambridge, had an undeniable attraction for the University (and for many other American campuses as well). The University's raw newness was seen as somehow softened by identification with time-honored ancient and medieval scholastic institutions. So, for whatever reasons, Gothic architectural design would be an enduring rule on the campus into the late 1950s, producing some of its most satisfying (if philosophically more doubtful) structures.

If 1915 was a seminal year for the campus in design terms, it also proved to be remarkable at a human level, because it was the year in which Henry Suzzallo became University president.

Raitt Hall
Photo: Stewart Hopkins

CHAPTER THREE

Suzzallo's "University of a Thousand Years"

HENRY SUZZALLO'S ASCENSION TO THE PRESIDENCY OF THE UNIVERSITY

launched eleven years of achievement under the leadership of a man with abilities and ambitions happily commensurate with the University's own circumstances and aspirations—and a man with whom Carl Gould established a notably symbiotic relationship. With the Regents Plan in place, the financing of a building program established, a rapidly growing regional population, and the enthusiastic leadership of a president with campus development in mind, paper dreams were suddenly given the opportunity to take form in physical reality.

Circumstances in fact demanded some sort of initiative. The University's inheritance from the AYPE had proved to be something of an embarrassment. There were five permanent buildings (paid for by the state), but there was also a scattering of temporary structures that were showily but flimsily built for a fleeting life that had been unexpectedly prolonged for University purposes. These temporary structures were deteriorating and required expensive repairs, but they were also an excuse for the legislature to withhold construction funds for their permanent replacements. As early as 1914, the University bursar had complained about the generally inferior level of University facilities, its overcrowded permanent buildings, plus AYPE "shacks, fast crumbling and deteriorating." He asked the legislature if it realized that since 1893 the state had given the University only $175,000 directly from state taxes for buildings and construction. Thus, Suzzallo had a fertile field waiting to be plowed in the interest of campus construction, as historian and professor Charles M. Gates noted in his University history:

> [Suzzallo] sought to expedite the building schedule as much as possible, and regularly presented the institution's needs to the legislature in the strongest terms. He was persuaded, however, that it was more important to build well than to build quickly. His concept was of a "Univer-

LEFT: Carl Gould's cathedral, the Smith Room, is in the south-facing wing of Suzzallo Library, built in 1935.
Photo: Stewart Hopkins
ABOVE: Henry Suzzallo, University of Washington president, 1915–1926
Photo: University of Washington Libraries, Special Collections and Preservation Division
RIGHT: Post-AYPE campus decay, 1915
Photo: University of Washington Libraries, Special Collections and Preservation Division

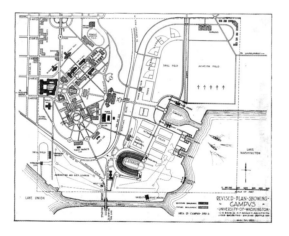

sity of a Thousand Years," hence each structure should be a monument, and a worthy one.

One of Suzzallo's first moves was to reorganize the campus committee formed to advise him in carrying out the Regents Plan, setting up a new membership with Carl Gould as its chairman. The committee, which included such campus luminaries as Edmond Meany, Herbert T. Condon, and Vernon Parrington, met for the first time on November 22, 1915. The legislature had established a system of earmarking money specifically for the University's building fund: construction funding would be based on receipts from tuition and from rentals of the downtown campus properties (for which a buyer had never been found), augmented by tax fund appropriations. As Gates would observe, this "made it possible for the University to plan and schedule new permanent structures at the rate of approximately one every eighteen months. The availability of such funds for plant development represented a tremendous vitalizing force which breathed new life into the institution as a whole and quite transformed the campus."

America's entry into the First World War disrupted campus life. Many areas of the campus were assigned to military purposes and construction, much of the latter cheaply built. Once these structures were standing, their destruction would be extremely difficult to rationalize (several are still in existence today!). It was also in 1917 that the Lake Washington Ship Canal was completed; the lake was lowered by 8.8 feet, and fill from the dredging added approximately one hundred acres to the campus.

With the end of the war, the focus was once again on building to meet the expanding demands of a burgeoning university. Efforts centered on development of the newly configured Liberal Arts Quad, which had already been started in 1916 with the collegiate-Gothic Home Economics Building (now Raitt Hall), a construction sequence that quickly moved on to Commerce Hall (1917) and Philosophy Hall (1920, now jointly known as Savery Hall), Education Hall (1922, now Miller Hall), Condon Hall (1932, now Gowen Hall), and Smith Hall (1939). These as well as the first wing of the new library (1926, now Suzzallo Library) were all in various interpretations of collegiate Gothic (and all except Condon Hall were designed by Bebb and Gould). The quad's closure would not be completed until after the Second World War.

The completion of the new library was especially central to meeting the University's education and physical design goals, but for Suzzallo those were perhaps transcended by the symbolic goals he set for the building. As his personal secretary, Lillian Brown Getty, was later to recall, "One of [Suzzallo's] dreams for the University was to have a splendidly equipped library housed in a suitable building.

TOP RIGHT: Parrington Hall and Denny Hall, in the distance, suffered from neglect following the AYPE.
Photo: University of Washington Libraries, Special Collections and Preservation Division
TOP LEFT: Bebb and Gould sketch of Commerce Hall and Philosophy Hall (now jointly known as Savery Hall)
Photo: University of Washington Libraries, Special Collections and Preservation Division
ABOVE: Bebb and Gould campus plan, 1920
Photo: University of Washington Libraries, Special Collections and Preservation Division

RIGHT: The original Bebb and Gould plan for the University's library and Central Plaza, 1925
Photo: University of Washington Libraries, Special Collections and Preservation Division
BELOW: In 1933, the University of Washington Library was renamed Suzzallo Library.
Photo: University of Washington Libraries, Special Collections and Preservation Division
OVERLEAF: Suzzallo Library
Photo: Stewart Hopkins

...The library was to be the monumental building on the campus." On the completion of its first phase of construction in 1926, its collegiate-Gothic presence surely met his ambitions. Thus the postwar library plus the University's newly occupied quad buildings, with their patterned brick of tawny rose through soft browns to the creams of terra-cotta trim, the gray of cast stone, and the sea greens of roof slate, established a palette of materials and color that is effectively reasserting itself in present-day construction.

During these years another campus goal was made more explicit, one that would establish connections—both functionally and ceremonially—with the larger community. Its origins had been with Suzzallo, who wrote in 1924 that he wanted a more appropriate approach from the city and, specifically, from University Bridge to the campus, a replacement for the ordinary street grid that was clumsily fulfilling that role. The proposal that met with the most favor was that of a broad avenue running from Tenth to Fifteenth avenues Northeast between Northeast Fortieth and Northeast Forty-first streets. The plan had been drawn up by Gould, endorsed by the Board of Regents, and backed by the University Commercial Club.

In a letter to the chairman of the regents' Building and Grounds Committee, Suzzallo discussed the University plan and the traffic congestion around the campus, including comments specifically pertaining to the westerly approach. According to Suzzallo, the entire architectural scheme of the University implied that there should be an approach to the Auditorium [Meany Hall] and Main Quad [Central Plaza] that would be located between East Fortieth and East Forty-first on axis with a large campus entrance court. A 1923 Bebb and Gould campus plan perspective and subsequent plans show such an approach, but it was many years before this idea reached fruition.

However, by 1934, Bebb and Gould as the University's "supervising architects" were asked by the regents to update the 1915 Regents Plan. The firm's resulting 1935 report reviewed the 1915 plan and recommended changes. The report began by reaffirming the basic design principles of earlier plans: "These [Liberal Arts, Science, and Central] quads are the center of academic life and the institution and the key to

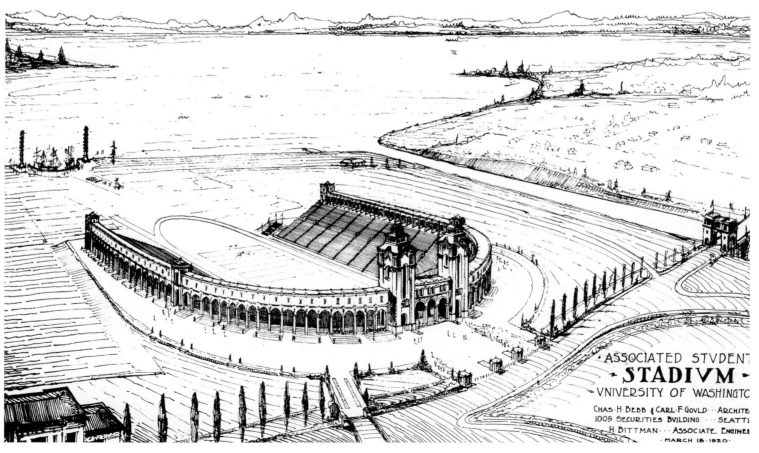

ASSOCIATED STVDENT
· STADIVM ·
VNIVERSITY OF WASHINGTO
CHAS·H·BEBB & CARL·F·GOVLD···ARCHITE
1005 SECURITIES BVILDING ···SEATTL
H·BITTMAN···ASSOCIATE ENGINEE
·MARCH 18·1920·

the entire campus plan," and they established the architectural style as Tudor or collegiate Gothic and determined the materials and color scheme necessary to a homogeneous future development.

The 1935 Plan then recommended certain modifications, such as lowering the building densities south of Science Quad and slightly altering building configuration at the easterly end of Liberal Arts Quad. It also called for some adjustments that eventually informed major campus development decisions (but not until after World War II): the location of a comprehensive student union building due east of Suzzallo Library, the assignment of the campus golf course south of Northeast Pacific Street to a health sciences complex, and the development of the northeasterly campus ridge above and paralleling Montlake Boulevard for student housing as well as abandonment of the 1915 assignment of the northwest campus corner to men's dorms. But the basic personality of the Regents Plan was fundamentally reaffirmed by its 1935 successor.

Landscaping

One of the campus glories has always been its landscaping; after all, part of Meany's rationale in support of such a large land acquisition for University purposes had been

ABOVE: Hutchinson Hall was designed by Bebb and Gould and built in 1927.
Photo: University of Washington Libraries, Special Collections and Preservation Division
RIGHT: Rainier Vista landscaping below Frosh Pond
Photo: University of Washington Libraries, Special Collections and Preservation Division

TOP: Johnson Hall (left) and Physics Hall were designed by John Graham and built in 1930 and 1928, respectively.
Photo: The Seattle Times, photo archive
ABOVE: In 1946, following World War II and passage of the GI Bill, student enrollment taxed the University's facilities beyond their capacity.
Photo: University of Washington Libraries, Special Collections and Preservation Division
RIGHT: Hansee Hall was built with WPA funds in 1936. It housed Navy and Marine officer candidates during World War II.
Photo: Stewart Hopkins

its potential for arboretum development. Toward that end, he had instigated the appointment of Henry H. Hindshaw as landscape architect for the University and included as an additional duty that of "Curator of the Arboretum." Meany also initiated a dynamic program not only to save trees and shrubs appropriate to the beautification of the campus but also to import and nurture a number of trees not originally found there such as sequoias, tulip poplars, eastern maples, Oregon ashes, and monkey puzzles. Policy statements by the regents also suggested their interest in principle in campus landscape planning. In 1919, a regents' statement on procedures for governing campus construction included a request that the University employ a landscape specialist, landscape gardener, and nurseryman, whose plans would be required to conform to the general plan of the campus.

But this request seems to have been only good intentions. There are fleeting references in the records to Meany's Hindshaw, but the University did not make a substantial commitment to a landscape architect for the campus until the 1930s, when it hired a Harvard graduate named Butler S. Sturtevant. Sturtevant's career before coming to the Pacific Northwest had been mostly in designing private estates and gardens on the East Coast. By 1928, he was working for a range of Seattle-area clients and was associated with a number of Seattle architects, including Bebb and Gould. Gould recommended him to the University as a landscape architect, a staff position he held from 1931 to 1939. Among the drawings bearing his name are 1936 designs for the junction of Rainier Vista and "Central Walk" (Stevens Way) with Bebb and Gould; a walk and grading design west of the new Women's Dorm (1936); the Rainier Vista approach and surrounds for Frosh Pond (1936); planting plans for Hutchinson Hall and nearby road realignments (1938); and drawings for the southerly closure of Rainier Vista. But it is uncertain how much resulted from his proposals. Too often in these years, when a building or site change occurred on campus, the policy was simply to assign grounds crews the tasks of repair and landscaping, rather than having the continuous counsel of landscape professionals, which would have ensured the consistent quality of this aspect of the campus scene.

During the World War II years, plans for new buildings and landscaping were put on hold. Economists expected the postwar years to begin with a recession, but they were wrong. By the spring term of 1946 the University's campus was bursting with returning GIs looking for university degrees, and temporary classrooms and living quarters were hurriedly being placed on every vacant, flat site the University could find.

The Postwar Campus Evolution and Charles E. Odegaard

SINCE THE WAR, THE UNIVERSITY'S CAMPUS HAS BECOME DENSER

in development and much larger in expanse; the latter was the result of further acquisitions at both the east and the southwest. The challenge again was to bring to these areas (especially the newer ones) a coordinated unity of design compatible with what had been established on the Central Campus. But the immediate postwar impact was a sharp increase in enrollment and the consequent demands for the expansion of physical space to accommodate it. The GI Bill opened the way for a flood of returning veterans who saw in its largess a whole new world of possibilities to which a university education was the key. Their presence, plus more versatile funding potentials—a more generous legislature, federal government sources, and private support—inspired a cornucopia of possibilities, many of which translated into new campus construction.

Surely the most profound of those changes was the inauguration of the medical school. Both law and medicine had been proposed as University programs by the regents in 1884, but they had failed to get legislative support. Law, which had originally been located on the University's downtown campus, found its way onto the campus in 1899, while medicine, even as a program, was forced to wait until 1946.

When medicine did join the University family, it did so with panache. The legislature and University were determined that if they made such a substantial venture they would aim for the top, and to a remarkable degree they succeeded. With significant investment in facilities, faculty, and staff, the health sciences programs quickly attained the top ranks in the pecking order of the medical education world; in recent years the ranks of Nobel laureates have included three members of the University medical faculty.

Included in the new health sciences complex were schools of medicine, dentistry, and nursing, and a three hundred–bed teaching hospital. The construction investment in these programs, with their specialized laboratories, classrooms, support facilities, and administrative quarters, exceeded $30 million by the early second decade of its existence. And that momentum has never ceased. Health sciences construction has expanded from the site assigned to it by the 1935 Plan to an enormous complex of linked buildings—sprawling from near the Montlake Bridge westward below Northeast Pacific Street to Fifteenth Avenue Northeast—whose interiors are a warren of halls leading off in multitudinous directions. Of the 13.9 million square feet of today's campus construction, some 3.162 million square feet (23 percent) of it is for the health sciences. The very mass and density of the complex have made it extremely difficult for the University to maintain some semblance of campus open space and accessibility to the pleasures of the shoreline along the canal and Portage Bay. In such efforts a number of design studies have been made, including those by the Seattle firms of NBBJ and Jones and Jones, and the coordination of these studies with planning for the southwest sector of the campus is helping to vitalize this southerly shoreline as a University treasure.

LEFT: Named for Dr. David C. Hall, Hall Health Center was built in part with WPA funds and opened in 1936.
Photo: Stewart Hopkins
ABOVE: Fall enrollment swelled following World War II from 5,943 in 1944 to 9,029 in 1945, and 15,594 by 1946.
Photo: University of Washington Libraries, Special Collections and Preservation Division

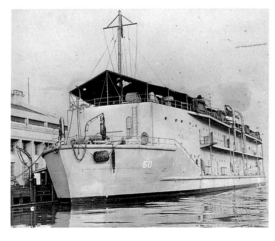

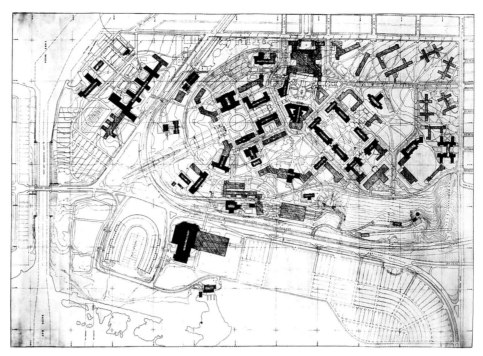

TOP LEFT: In 1945 temporary classrooms were placed around the campus, then filled with returning GIs.
Photo: University of Washington Libraries, Special Collections and Preservation Division
CENTER: After World War II, housing for married students was constructed around the campus perimeter.
Photo: University of Washington Libraries, Special Collections and Preservation Division
BOTTOM: A surplus Navy ship was moored just west of the Montlake cut and used as dormitory and classroom space.
Photo: MOHAI, The PI Collection
TOP RIGHT: Campus plan, 1949
Photo: University of Washington Libraries, Special Collections and Preservation Division

In the tradition of periodic review established by Bebb and Gould's 1935 Plan, the same firm (by then known as Jones and Bindon) was asked by the regents to revise and update the University's basic plan—a timely decision in light of the heavy expansionist pressures the campus was facing. The result was the 1948 Plan. Like its 1935 predecessor, the revised Regents Plan gained a willing adherence, though it was now scaled to a projected enrollment of twenty-five thousand. The plan's first-priority recommendation was the acquisition of the Northlake area, substantial acreage south of Northeast Fortieth Street between Fifteenth Avenue Northeast and Eleventh Avenue Northeast, and Northeast Pacific Street. The plan also restated support for the concept of a University boulevard as the westerly approach to the campus.

The plan made some further recommendations for increasing the density of development, especially surrounding Science Quad, but mostly it reaffirmed provisions in the 1935 Plan, such as the northeast ridge of dormitories, the closing in of the northeasterly end of Liberal Arts Quad, and the expansion of construction surrounding old Meany Hall.

All of these proposals were intended to provide facilities to match the expansion of programs and enrollment already accomplished or soon to be expected. The plan also recommended acquisition of the then-empty land east of the railroad right-of-way (now the Burke-Gilman Trail) to Union Bay Place and north of Northeast Forty-fifth Street; the University acquired the most westerly portion of the site for a large service building, but the rest was acquired by others for development as a shopping center and similar uses.

Completion of the 1948 Plan was timely, because the 1950s were to be a period of enormous activity. The first phase, fueled by a construction budget in excess of $21.5 million, was expected to serve a myriad of specialized uses, and included costly laboratories, library expansion, new classroom buildings, the Administration Building, and the new Student Union Building (the HUB). Each addition found its place in the campus plan, some more felicitously than others. In this postwar period, those dollars bought almost 1.2 million square feet of academic floor space, nearly doubling what the University had had before the war.

One of the plan's more ostentatious completions was Campus Parkway, the realization of Suzzallo's dream of the 1920s for a more ceremonial connection between the north end of University Bridge and the campus. Completed in 1953, this east-west approach—in the boulevard manner with a planting-strip divider—was on axis awkwardly aimed at the backside of Meany Hall. This fact, together with the con-

TOP: The University of Washington School of Medicine was established in 1946. Its rapid growth is shown in this 1948 aerial of the University campus.
Photo: University of Washington Libraries, Special Collections and Preservation Division
ABOVE: Charles E. Odegaard, University of Washington president, 1958–1973
Photo: University of Washington, News and Information

tinuing use of the utilitarian Northeast Fortieth Street entrance (a holdover from the AYPE plan) and a tangle of utility poles and lines, has deprived the Parkway of its intended ceremonial panache. Nor has it been helped by the disheveled planting of trees at the western end, remnants of a 1961 international forestry conference on campus.

Charles E. Odegaard

The 1950s also brought to the campus something more than physical changes; they brought President Charles E. Odegaard, another of those towering figures who, like Suzzallo, would be a force that influenced all phases of University life. Odegaard was a man whose talents and leadership were both scholarly and administrative. His arrival in August 1958 initiated or paralleled University developments of almost unprecedented impact. With Odegaard also came his commitment to the campus environment, in which he was ably assisted by the late Ernest M. Conrad, '40, his vice president for business and finance. Conrad shared Suzzallo's insistence on both practical and esthetic quality for this University of a Thousand Years. Much of the next phase of campus development was initiated or at least nurtured by Odegaard's interest and often personal involvement during the years of his presidency, which ended with his retirement in 1973. The University's teaching and research space more than doubled on his watch.

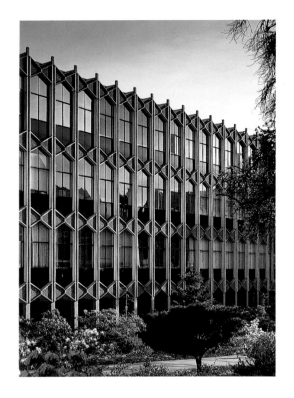

Although it had been established the year before Odegaard's arrival on campus, the University Architectural Commission came into its own through his continuing support and, often, his direct participation in its activities. The commission—ordinarily chaired by the dean of the College of Arts and Sciences—is composed of an imposing array of professionals (some with national and international reputations), including Minoru Yamasaki, William Wurster, Hideo Sasaki, James Ingo Freed, Norman Pfeiffer, Robert Frasca, Laurie Olin, and Peter Walker. It represents the University as client in advising the regents on architectural matters, primarily selecting architects and other design professionals and critiquing their submittals. A University architect was also appointed in 1957 and given staff support. These developments have given cohesiveness and continuity to the changes on campus.

The influence of the commission was particularly significant because of nationwide changes in the architectural profession that had local repercussions, including the demise of collegiate Gothic as the campus design standard. One observer of the change explained that the main reason why the modern supplanted the Gothic on campus was not cost, but rather a shift in attitudes of the University officials in charge of the campus plan and a fundamental shift in the philosophies and attitudes of the architects themselves. As one of the practitioners affected by the revolution observed, after World War II it became more difficult to consistently maintain that (collegiate-Gothic) rigid design control. "The philosophies of modern architectural design did not accept eclecticism, and the university's role as a leader in teaching and research was not consistent with facade design and construction methods developed centuries earlier."

The modernists won. The Architectural Commission was charged with making design judgments to replace the discredited collegiate-Gothic formula. Initial results, in the light of hindsight, were not reassuring: Sieg and MacKenzie halls (both 1960), and Balmer Hall and an addition to Suzzallo Library (both 1962). Ironically, Sieg Hall, now most people's choice as least welcome of the genre, was approvingly featured on the cover of a national architectural journal at the time of its completion.

In the meantime, the University architect's office was at work on what would become the 1962 General Development Plan. In preparation for it, special consultants were brought in to offer their insights. One of these was UW graduate Paul Thiry, a local architect with a national reputation and the chief architect of Seattle's 1962 World's Fair. He had considerable city-planning experience, having served as a member of the Seattle City Planning Commission in the late 1950s. Perhaps for that reason, his report brought unprecedented scope, placing the campus within an areawide, even regional, context, especially with respect to transportation. As for the

In the 1990s, bicycles became the quickest means of on-campus transportation.
Photo: Loyd Heath

campus itself, he reported that if the University was to survive its present traffic problems, it was essential to control the movement of vehicles and people. He recommended that traffic be diverted to the peripheral roadways, entering the campus only at designated locations.

Thiry's report would therefore propose a system of several campus circumferential and interior service routes, as well as parking facilities, including an underground location at Central Plaza. He reaffirmed the 1948 Plan's recommendation to acquire the Northlake area, noting that current federal urban-renewal legislation would assist the University in that effort. Thiry also advocated open spaces and expansion of the Central Plaza concept. In the latter, Thiry's recommendations were to be refined by the work of other consultants. The firm of Walker and McGough of Spokane was asked by the University in 1962 "to consider planning concepts and to develop a plan for the Central Campus for future development." Their study— the first to embrace the principles of the emerging discipline of urban design for the campus—was to include such matters as building character, spatial relationships between buildings, tree and shrubbery masses, analysis of open-space characteristics, and vistas. Their analysis and drawings for Central Plaza were to be key to what eventually developed there.

Much of what came out of these consultants' reports was folded into the 1962 Development Plan, which incorporated many of the proposals of earlier plans all the way back to the Regents Plan of 1915 but recognized the broader range of influences both on the campus and beyond, particularly the automobile, its movements, and its parking (14,500 spaces were included in Thiry's plan). The plan also proposed that the University seize the opportunity represented by the Northlake properties; it justified their acquisition and provided a long-range plan for their development as required by federal urban-renewal provisions. The plan was reviewed and approved by the University planning office, the regents, and also the City Planning Commission.

The latter was a precedent for a trend that was soon to follow. The resulting Northlake Urban Renewal Plan was, in due course, the basis for the University's addition of thirty-four acres to its campus, extending all the way to Portage Bay (though this was not accomplished without considerable resistance from the community, the basis for the University's continuing awkward relationships with some of its neighbors).

A Landscaping Renaissance

Although the landscape of the campus site was one of the things that had attracted Meany to it, this aspect of campus development received only sporadic attention for many years. There were brief episodes in which gardeners had been proposed but probably served only as grounds workers.

At the time of the AYPE, the Olmsted firm had recommended that the University do something more substantial in its landscape program, but the regents replied that "there are absolutely no funds at our disposal that can be appropriated for that purpose." Except for the period in the 1930s when Butler Sturtevant was the landscape architect, it seems the ordinary practice after new campus construction was to assign grounds people to do whatever was necessary to heal the site wounds with available plantings.

This practice changed in the 1960s, when the California landscape architect Lawrence Halprin was hired to collaborate with both Thiry and Walker and McGough on their studies. In 1969 the University established a new Campus Planning Office, whose staff included not only professional planners but also a landscape architect. This was followed in 1970 by creation of the Advisory Committee on University Landscaping and Planting (recently given the less pretentious name of University Landscape Advisory Committee), which fills a role similar to that of the Architectural Commission. Its members are representatives from the various programs and activities on campus related to landscape issues and concerns. In its advisory role to the University administration, it examines and critiques any site planning and landscape issues that evolve through campus development processes—new construction, remodelings, planting plans, and the like. These days, construction contracts include landscape consultants and their proposals as an integral part of the process. Recent outstanding projects that have resulted from this policy are the Allen Library and its relationship with Grant Lane and HUB Yard (1990), Grieg Garden (also 1990), the Physics/Astronomy Building (1994), and the just-completed Chemistry Building addition (1995).

ABOVE: Campus landscape detail
Photo: Loyd Heath
OVERLEAF: Grieg Garden
Photo: Stewart Hopkins

TOP: Early conceptual drawing of campus buildings, such as this one of the Student Union Building, included open spaces and attention to landscape design.
Photo: The Seattle Times, *photo archive*
ABOVE: 1939 placement of Larado Taft's bronze George Washington Monument
Photo: University of Washington Libraries, Special Collections and Preservation Division
RIGHT: George Washington Monument
Photo: Randy Wells/Tony Stone Images

The campus is thus becoming enriched as a landscape environment. For example, besides the remnants of the original campus forest, such as the grove just south of Frosh Pond (along Island Lane), major plantings have been added over the years: large evergreen and deciduous species, smaller-scaled flowering cherries and crab apples, woody shrubs such as rhododendrons and azaleas, and seasonal plantings at several of the campus entrances and elsewhere that bring splendid color to the campus. These developments are for more than looks: the campus is used increasingly as a teaching tool. In response to the need for a clear design program and the desire for greater diversity in plant selection, a new plant association plan was developed in 1990. It divided the campus into fourteen geographic zones, some of whose titles suggest the plan's intent: United States Atlantic Coast Flora, Conifer Forest and Temperate Sub Story of Shrubs and Herbaceous Plants Native to the Pacific Northwest, Eurasian Flora, United States Pacific Coast Flora. The springtime campus is a special glory when its plantings come into full bloom.

Art on Campus

Art on the campus is another form of its enrichment. The first ambitious efforts in this direction, which came as adjuncts of the AYPE, were the bronze George Washington Monument by Larado Taft, one of the major American sculptors at the turn of the century, and two Finn H. Frolich pieces—one of Edvard Grieg, the other of James J. Hill. After the exposition, all three works found permanent places on the campus. A long dry period followed. When new sculpture appeared, it was confined to those pieces incorporated into the building designs themselves. Gould very much encouraged this and included it in his designs for new buildings in Liberal Arts Quad and especially the library. That tradition reappears in the later work of various other sculptors such as Alan Clark, Dudley Pratt, and Everett DuPen on postwar buildings of the 1940s and after.

The gift of Barnett Newman's *Broken Obelisk* was an inspired freestanding addition to the central quad in 1971, and similar smaller pieces have appeared subsequently: Philip Levine's *Dancer with a Flat Hat*, on a stair landing leading to Schmitz Hall; and a small fountain by George Tsutakawa and a charming granite Japanese lantern, both found in the MacKenzie/Balmer halls complex.

A more ambitious piece of art is the untitled environmental design by Mary Miss, an assemblage of garden components in a glade east of health sciences. East across Montlake Boulevard beyond the Canoehouse is the Rollback Bench, designed by Christy Rupp. The nearby Climbing Rock, while not meant as sculpture, nevertheless deserves mention as a handsome object in the landscape, its surfaces often peopled by climbers in various precarious positions.

To encourage increasing commitment to such campus additions, both without and within University buildings, a Public Arts Program and its arts administrator, along with the state's ½ Percent for Art funding, are now permanent features of University policy.

Community Participation

One of the significant new forces shaping campus policies and development is the participation of the larger community in University decisions. In an earlier day, in matters affecting the campus, the University, along with the legislature and regents, went about its business essentially as a free agent. This is no longer true. Beginning with the Northlake urban-renewal episode, recent years have found neighborhood, city, state, and federal government all at the planning table, each with its own concerns and requirements to be accommodated in University planning considerations.

LEFT: "Art" on campus is sometimes a part of its architecture. Shown is the main entrance to Guggenheim Hall.
Photo: Loyd Heath
ABOVE: Father Neptune is part of the east gable of the Administration Building, which was completed in 1949.
Photo: Loyd Heath
RIGHT: George Tsutakawa's *Fountain of Reflection*
Photo: Loyd Heath

Current requirements call for the University to seek city building permits, agree to set boundaries for University properties, ensure state review of major projects and development plans (SEPA), develop environmental impact statements, and observe shoreline-protection regulations.

There are other aspects of contemporary life and the campus environment in which the University has the community in mind. In response to new standards for accessibility to its facilities, both the campus itself and its buildings have undergone substantial revisions to accommodate wheelchairs both outside and in. A notable example of the former is where Central Plaza opens on the southeast to Rainier Vista. A new ramp was worked ingeniously into the existing stairs and wall by Garnett Schorr Architects as part of a 1992 renovation of the Administration Building, without violating the design quality of that location between Suzzallo Library and the Administration Building.

Concerns for personal safety on campus have also resulted in an expanded system of standard but dignified lighting fixtures throughout the campus for greater visibility. Landscape policy for similar reasons has resulted in plant pruning practices to maintain the perception and reality of a secure and accessible campus.

Another new phenomenon is the presence of design professionals from out of state doing work on campus. In the past, campus designers almost always were Seattle practitioners, or at least from within the state. But this has been changed by current national economics and the nature of architectural practice. In times when building activity is down in one part of the country, professionals in the field are likely to look elsewhere. This versatility is encouraged by modern technology—fax machines, computers, e-mail, cross-country air service—which facilitates practice on a national, even international, scale. Understandably, local architects are disturbed by this development (though possibly also expanding their own practices to distant sites). But it does explain why the University now finds working on its campus a number of national luminaries, including Romaldo Giurgola, Cesar Pelli, Charles Moore (all AIA Gold Medalists), Edward Larrabee Barnes, Michael McKinney, and Charles Gwathmey, often in association with such substantial local firms as TRA, NBBJ, Loschky Marquardt and Nesholm, and Hewitt Isley.

The Odegaard years saw a heady expansion of students, faculty, staff, research, resources, and facilities. No longer a regional institution, the University had become one of national prominence, establishing a momentum that continues to this day.

CHAPTER FIVE

William P. Gerberding and the Politics of Growth

WHEN WILLIAM P. GERBERDING CAME TO THE UNIVERSITY AS PRESIDENT

in 1979, he introduced another period of enormous change that would leave its mark on campus development. President Gerberding arrived with high ambitions for the University's academic programs and national reputation, and the sixteen years of his tenure have left impressive indices of the University's success under his administration: "glowing reports" in a recent evaluation of higher-education institutions; listing as one of the top schools in the country in the national press; consistent ranking among the top two or three American universities receiving federal research funds; grades of A in "virtually every category" from an institutional survey of seven western states; and listing as one of the best values in education in the U.S. in a 1994 *U.S. News & World Report*.

The president was also markedly successful in his dealings with the legislature, University alumni, and the general community. Even in some difficult budgetary times, the University has been reasonably well treated, and its recent five-year Campaign for Washington raised $284 million, well above its target. Gerberding's message: the University is a major resource for the state and deserves nurturing and support to fulfill that role.

The message was tested early. A disturbing development faced the University in the mid-1980s, when a study of its aging science and engineering facilities found that they were out-of-date for the requirements of contemporary teaching and research. Without immediate action, the position of the University in those disciplines would be seriously jeopardized. Taking the case to the legislature, the administration convinced the state's elected officials of the need for targeted funding. The result was legislative authorization for five major new projects: the Physics/Astronomy Building, the Chemistry Building addition, the Electrical Engineering/Computer Sciences Building, and two large additions to the health sciences complex. These projects, plus the new Allen Library (partially financed by a $10 million gift from Paul Allen), not only helped meet the demands of those programs but also demonstrated the support the University receives from the legislature and the state.

All these projects have benefited greatly from Gerberding's choice, in 1987, of Tallman Trask III as executive vice president. A man with a real enthusiasm for the campus, Trask has participated actively in its development and has been the main agent of the Gerberding administration's impact on the campus environment.

In this era of complex finance, the failure of the University to sell the old downtown campus, both in 1891 and subsequently, has proven to be a benefit. Those ten acres now make the University the owner of a major tract of land and high-rise buildings in downtown Seattle's commercial heart—the Metropolitan Tract—whose income over the years has been valuable for campus development, both in land acquisitions and new building construction.

LEFT: The Allen Library
Photo: Jeff Zaruba
ABOVE: Dr. William P. Gerberding, University of Washington president, 1979–1995
Photo: Mary Levin, University of Washington, News and Information
OVERLEAF: Anderson Hall
Photo: Stewart Hopkins

Between 1962 and 1994 there have been eighty major architectural projects on the campus, twenty-eight of those during Gerberding's tenure. All of this construction demonstrates the complexities of contemporary finance in University projects. In a simpler age, the University paid for its buildings out of either its own funds or those received from the legislature. This pattern was broken in 1925, when a gift from alumni financed the memorial pylons marking the University's Seventeenth Avenue Northeast entrance, and Agnes H. Anderson bequeathed $260,000 for Anderson Hall. By 1940, there had been only four additional gifts of a similar nature from foundations or individuals. But those latter years included a new resource, Public Works Administration funding from the federal government, whose presence on the postwar campus would loom much larger. In addition, a more substantial base of private participants had developed: foundations, businesses, industrial organizations and corporations, and individuals, adding to the pot from which building funds were drawn.

The manipulation of all this funding is a skill that calls for considerable maneuvering. A single project can find University administrators juggling funds from a variety of diverse sources: state appropriations; University-generated funds, including those from Metropolitan Tract leases; the sale of bonds, to be repaid from future federal research grants; challenge gifts (dollars given if matched with equal donations from other sources); and less-restrictive private donations—all of which can be part of a complex puzzle that requires deftness to capture its maximum potential.

In looking at current design policies on campus, as represented by recent projects, one discovers a recurring and welcome concern: the theme of campus design. The Walker and McGough study was a harbinger of this trend. Present design approaches and the review processes demonstrate a significant inclination in that direction. A campus by its very nature encourages that direction, but the concept is not necessarily honored in practice. Happily, it is honored on this campus. That clearly is the message in a sequence of projects that substantially demonstrate this priority: Allen Library, the Physics/Astronomy Building, the Chemistry Building addition, the Electrical Engineering/Computer Sciences Building, and (in design) the Business Administration expansion. Each of these projects has been reviewed not only for the quality of its architecture but also for how it adds to and reinforces the design framework of the campus. Indeed, the Regents Plan is still with us!

An especially interesting exercise in campus design was the construction of the Triangle Garage, located at the base of Rainier Vista. The garage was carefully placed underground in order to avoid any violation of that sacred vista. If one needed any reminder that the neighbors do care about what happens on campus, it could be found in the furious reaction to a sign announcing the construction—the sign having failed to note that the garage was to be underground. The sign was quickly amended!

The primary example of a design approach to the campus is the completion of Central Plaza. First projected in the 1915 Regents Plan, the plaza continued through successive decades as something of a chimera—a dream anticipated but unrealized. The 1926 phase of Suzzallo Library and, later, the construction of the Administration Building (1949) signaled the University's good intentions; the Thiry and Walker and McGough reports understood its importance.

With the completion of Campus Parkway there was the promise as well of an important visual access eastward into the plaza that would be handsomely closed by Suzzallo Library's west facade. But the vista was blocked by the backside of old Meany Hall, whose presence was the main impediment to progress on Central Plaza. Then nature intervened. The 1965 earthquake made Meany structurally unsafe; it was condemned and, shortly thereafter, demolished.

ABOVE: The Physics/Astronomy Building interior is a blend of form and function.
Photo: Chris Eden/Eden Arts
BELOW: Included in the Cesar Pelli design of the Physics/Astronomy Building are stone castings of physical equations.
Photo: Mary Levin, University of Washington, News and Information

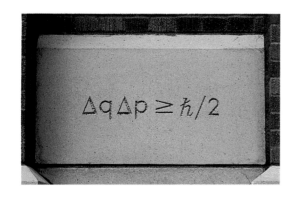

With much of the design future for the plaza already established, plans and construction moved rapidly forward, beginning in 1971 with the brick-paved plaza and its underground garage, followed by Kane Hall, Odegaard Undergraduate Library (1972), and the new Meany Hall (1974). Barnett Newman's *Broken Obelisk*—a gift of the Virginia Wright Foundation that looks as though it were designed specifically for its site, although it wasn't—adds an elegant grace note to this most urbane of campus open spaces.

So at last Suzzallo's and Gould's goal, declared in the Regents Plan, is in place. The arts and the sciences are linked by the University resources that support them both—libraries, lecture halls, performing arts, administration—resulting in an environmental response to an intellectual concept. Central Plaza's stark presence is never likely to be an object of campus affection among a public that—with some justification—is enamored of the lawns and cherry trees of Liberal Arts Quad. Nevertheless, the campus is enriched by its variety of open spaces.

There is now on campus another design redirection, nothing as revolutionary as the abandonment of collegiate Gothic in the late 1950s, but one much closer in its values to collegiate Gothic than that style's initial successor. Called "contextualism," the new approach calls for the designer to prepare for a project by analyzing its site in order to discover qualities and elements that can inform the design and assist it in establishing a compatible relationship with its surroundings. The designer

University of Washington Canoehouse
Photo: University of Washington Libraries, Special Collections and Preservation Division

seeks to reinforce or enhance and perhaps expand that relationship. Not an abandonment of modernism, contextualism looks for materials, patterns, forms, and details that evoke a cooperative association with a building's neighbors while retaining its essential independence, in the modern tradition. One campus example is the Allen Library, which has picked up certain clues from the library's Bebb and Gould wings: materials, patterning, module, and some details. (Its success, however, lies far more in its urban design relationships to Grant Lane and HUB Yard than in its architecture.)

Much better examples are provided by both the Physics/Astronomy Building and the Chemistry Building addition, whose designs exercise considerably more independence, yet are comfortable within the context of campus traditions and add wonderfully to the campus design framework. All this is reassuring to those who see the campus as an ensemble, a design community in which the whole becomes more important than the parts.

Another current campus enthusiasm that deserves honor is the emergence of historic preservation as an environmental value. Interesting to observe, in light of this preservationist momentum, is the fate of Denny Hall, which in the 1950s was actively considered for demolition and replacement—unthinkable today. Fortunately, this destruction did not occur, but the interior mutilations that followed would surely have been handled more sympathetically under present practices.

A more thoughtful approach is the one taken in 1987 for the rehabilitation of AYPE's old Fine Arts Building, now Architecture Hall. Originally intending only to improve the building's accessibility and meet code requirements, the University decided, instead, to do a more thorough job, with very satisfying results. There are now on campus a number of historic buildings that have the protection of being

listed on the Washington State Register of Historic Places. Besides Denny Hall there are Clark Hall, Lewis Hall, the Observatory, Parrington Hall, Architecture Hall, and the columns from the downtown University building, now relocated in the Sylvan Theater. In addition, the Canoehouse is on the National Register.

At the threshold of the twenty-first century, the University has become a world-class research institution that is deeply committed to undergraduate education. While it draws students from all fifty states and eighty-five countries, its special mission is serving the people of Washington State, home to 90 percent of its students. Its faculty includes four Nobel laureates and thirty-one members of the National Academy of Sciences, its libraries house more than five million bound volumes, and state-of-the-art buildings and facilities support its programs of teaching and research. Just 22 percent of the University's biennial budget of more than $2.3 billion is derived from state of Washington tax dollars, the balance coming from tuition and fees, grants and contracts, investments, sales and services, and such auxiliary units as residence halls, food services, and parking.

The University is a major recipient of grants and contract funds for research and training, maintaining its place in the nation among the top five institutions, both private and public, in receipt of federal awards. Every year since 1974, it has been number one in that category among public institutions. Its donation level from private voluntary sources currently ranks the University fourteenth nationally among all universities and fifth among public universities. Public and private grants amounted to more than $430 million in 1993–94. (Revenue sources have been roughly estimated at 20 percent from state general appropriations, 20 percent from the University's public land endowment, 20 percent from Metropolitan Tract income, 20 percent from tuition, 10 percent from the federal government, 5 percent from ASUW fees, and 5 percent from private, corporate, and foundation gifts.)

Sylvan Theater and columns
Photo: University of Washington, News and Information

Planning for the Future

Early in President Gerberding's tenure, a major construction project at University Hospital prompted legal challenges from the city. Besides questioning the adequacy of the project's environmental impact statement, the city chided the University for the "lack of an official master plan and mitigating measures to address the cumulative impacts of development" (according to a report by the University's planning office). The parties reached settlement by way of the 1983 City-University Agreement, an unprecedented compact that committed the University to prepare a master plan of future campus development for review and approval by the city.

This was the origin of the University's General Physical Development Plan for 1991–2001 (GPDP), a major effort of the 1980s embodied in a three-volume report that established the University's Master Plan policies and plans for land use, design, open space and landscape, site development, waterfront, transportation goals, and management, as well as a ten-year development program. After a prolonged review, the GPDP was approved in May 1992 by both the regents and the City Council.

Supplementary to the GPDP was a separate Southwest Campus Plan. That previously platted and developed part of the city had been acquired by the University in the 1960s, but a satisfactory design had never been devised. Its unimaginative grid and many existing buildings made it a challenge to establish any design compatibility between it and Central Campus. After a ten-year succession of efforts, a Southwest Campus Plan was in 1994 finally agreed to by both University and City.

With the approval of its GPDP, the University has set its course for moving into the twenty-first century, the culmination of a long succession of events that has given us a campus unique in the history of such efforts. Knowing now that history, turn to Part Two, there to find the personalities, circumstances, and aspirations that shaped the towers, the vistas, and the trees as they individually contribute toward this climactic glory: the campus of the University of Washington.

PART TWO

Campus Design, Architecture, and Landscape

THE UNIVERSITY OF WASHINGTON CAMPUS IS RICH IN A VARIETY of elements that give it space, form, pattern, and detail. Some of these elements are provided by nature; many more have been furnished by the people, policies, and practices of successive generations of campus shapers. The most obvious man-made elements are the buildings, with the history they represent and the variations of placement, form, and detail they provide. Much of campus history can be read in their names, thanks to the policy of naming buildings for faculty members or regents who have made significant intellectual contributions to the University's development (less often for individuals whose contribution was primarily monetary).

Then there is the landscape: a sloping site that gently flows southward to Portage Bay and the canal, abruptly edged to the east by heights overlooking the flatlands of east campus, with its athletic fields, parking, and distant Ecological Research Natural Area. Both nature and human effort have joined in enriching the campus with a palette of plantings: towering fir trees, pines, and giant redwoods; flowering trees and shrubs; sweeping lawns and colorful beds of seasonal flowerings. Some of the amenities are spatial and remind us of earlier times—the Sylvan Theater or its forested neighbor on the opposite side of Rainier Vista; others reclaimed from former parking lots now return as landscaped partners—the ivy-bedded base of Rainier Vista or the open lawns of Grieg Garden. Interspersed among all this are the spices of campus art, the finer-scaled elements that humanize the built world: a memorial plaque or a fountain, a freestanding sculptured figure or a satiric corniceline gargoyle, a stained-glass window or a class-memorial bench.

The design of the University of Washington campus—the plan with its hierarchy of axes, spaces, and forms, the patterns of its roads and paths, and the architecture and landscaping that give the plan its third dimension—reflects the changing tastes that the last hundred years have brought to the campus. Its plan still retains much of the grand monumentality of the turn-of-the-century City Beautiful movement that inspired it, via the Olmsted Brothers and their site design for the 1909 Alaska-Yukon-Pacific Exposition, later modified and extended by the 1915 Regents Plan. Through subsequent years, that plan has been adjusted to meet changing needs for an expanding University population, new construction, and transportation technology. But its design principles have been retained, proving their ongoing relevance to campus development.

No clear stylistic pattern was established by the first buildings: Denny Hall, a satisfying interpretation of the French Renaissance, brick and mortar with stone details; austere and plainspoken Lewis and Clark halls; and Parrington Hall, of no readily identified style. Not until the 1916 construction of the Home Economics Building (now Raitt Hall) as the first building of Liberal Arts Quad did the University venture into the collegiate-Gothic tradition to which it remained faithful (especially on upper campus) until the latter 1950s.

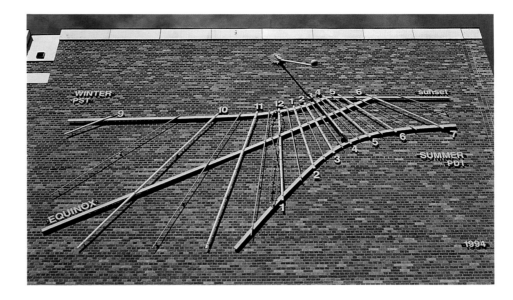

Thereafter, the regents allowed architectural modernism to find its place in campus design, with the varied results one now finds there. More recent campus construction is evidence of yet another trend noted earlier: contextualism, with its concern that new buildings recognize the ambience of their surroundings, thus reinforcing the design unity of the campus though at the possible risk of neglecting opportunities for more daring design innovation.

The campus landscape still retains areas reminiscent of its earliest days: natural groupings of trees and shrubs featuring a few older-growth trees mixed with woody plants and ground cover that might well have been there when the regents made that first survey trip of their new landholdings in 1893. But the bulk of today's campus landscape is the result of considerable effort to ensure that campus design and building placements are strengthened and beautified by plantings. Both native and non-native varieties are chosen for maximum visual and pedagogical effectiveness, as well as for horticultural versatility and richness. The wonderful spring display of Yoshino cherry trees (placed in the early 1960s in Liberal Arts Quad) and the more recently developed HUB Yard and Grieg Garden are handsome reminders of just how much a sustained landscape policy has glorified our campus environment. And underlying everything are the drama and grandeur of the campus plan, where each part of the ensemble finds its place in the overall scheme of spaces, vistas, and circumferential routes.

What follows is a more detailed appreciation of what the campus has become. It is written in the hope that these words and pictures will invite the reader to the campus itself, whose beauties are only truly revealed through personal experience.

CHAPTER SIX

North Campus

THE UNIVERSITY'S FIRST BUILDINGS ON ITS NEW CAMPUS WERE BUILT WELL

below its northern border along Northeast Forty-fifth. After the 1909 AYPE most of the University's buildings were constructed in the Central and South campuses, and since 1965 nothing has been built in North Campus, except for the Glenn Hughes Penthouse Theater, moved to this area in 1992 to make room for the Physics/Astronomy Building. Its older buildings and landscaped open spaces are a pleasing contrast to the other, more congested, campus regions.

Northwest Sector

Until the 1950s the northwest sector of the campus was almost entirely wooded or landscaped open space, and it is still the central campus sector of lowest-density development. Much of it is now assigned to parking, though plant screening protects the visitor from most of that visual blight. Aligned southerly from Seventeenth Avenue Northeast and opening off Northeast Forty-fifth Street is Memorial Gateway, which identifies this as the University's ceremonial entrance. Its two main pylons were placed there in 1928, financed by the senior classes of the previous ten years, with matching funds from the University. The pylons carry plaques with the names of University students who lost their lives in the First World War. (At least one nearby fraternity required that its pledges keep polished the names of its listed brothers.) In 1949 the outer pylons were added to complete the ensemble. The University signage between them is a recent addition. Seasonal planting beds, here and elsewhere on campus, add their visual welcome to the visitor.

Just east of the Gateway is the site of one of the campus's environmental tragedies. This was the location of the Chimes Tower, originally a wooden water tower built to serve the early University (there being no city water service at that time). It had been retrofitted for more inspirational purposes with the 1912 installation of a set of twelve chimes, a donation of regent A. J. Blethen, the *Seattle Times* publisher. The tradition of playing its bells began in 1918 with the appointment of George Bailey, '17, a blind pianist, and is in the memories of generations of students.

But the music was silenced on May 24, 1949, when a mysterious (and possibly arson-caused) fire destroyed the tower and its fifteen-thousand-pound carillon. The bells were replaced with a pallid substitute, an "electric carillon" whose keyboard in the basement of the Music Building was connected to a loudspeaker in Denny Hall's cupola. The 1995 installation of a new digital carillon system, all in a room atop Denny Hall, promises to improve the sound and revive the tradition of regular concerts ringing across the campus.

Aiming due south from Memorial Gateway, Memorial Way is one of the major axes of the campus. This and the other vistas and routes of the 1915 Regents Plan act as a spatial skeleton, connectors to the spaces and forms of the campus design. Memorial Way's fifty-eight bordering sycamores further memorialize the students lost

LEFT: Memorial Way
Photo: Loyd Heath
ABOVE: Memorial Gateway pylon
Photo: Stewart Hopkins

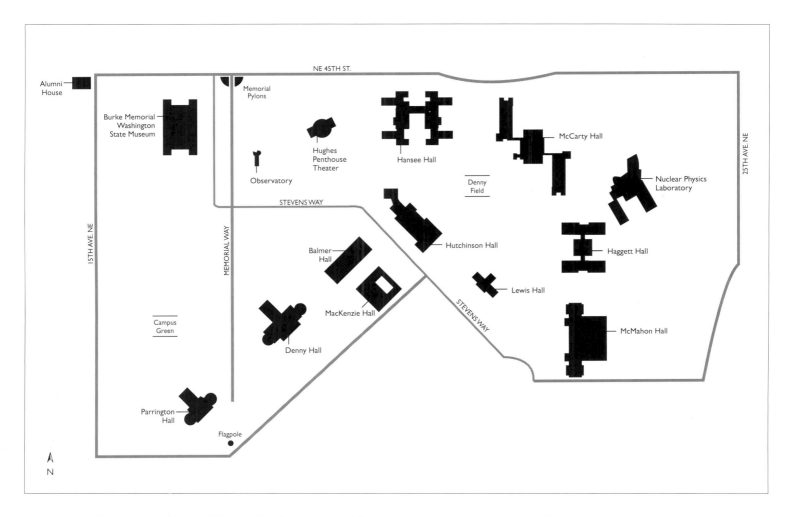

TOP: North Campus map
ABOVE LEFT: George Bailey before the Chimes Tower fire in 1949
Photo: The Seattle Times, photo archive
ABOVE RIGHT: The Observatory and Chimes Tower
Photo: University of Washington Libraries, Special Collections and Preservation Division
OPPOSITE: The Observatory
Photo: Stewart Hopkins

in the First World War—fifty-seven men and one woman. The dappled shade of the trees' canopy in spring and summer gives way to autumn's gold and winter's bareness, unfolding reminders of campus seasonal changes.

Immediately west of Memorial Way is Burke Memorial Washington State Museum, the oldest university museum in the West, founded in 1885. Major funding for the current building came in a bequest from the late Caroline McGilvra Burke in memory of her husband, Judge Thomas Burke (1849–1925), a pioneer civic leader of Seattle. It was supplemented by a state appropriation. Built to replace the museum's previous home (the former and dilapidated AYPE Washington State Pavilion, which

was declared unsafe and torn down in 1959), the Burke holds a noted Indian collection, as well as anthropology, geology, and zoology exhibits from mainland and island nations around the Pacific Rim. The building originally was designed around an interior two-story gallery, since built over for additional exhibit space. The tall totem poles once displayed in that gallery are now found on the grounds in front of the museum.

In the main-floor Burke Memorial Room is the fifteen-by-seven-foot "peacock window," one of the finest works of Louis Comfort Tiffany, formerly in the Seattle residence of Eliza Ferry Leary, daughter of Washington's first governor, Elisha Ferry. The museum also has a small lobby gift shop and The Boiserie, a coffee and pastry shop whose waxed pine wall panels (probably from the early eighteenth century) and carved white limestone chimneypiece were imported from France. At one time they were in the music room of the home of D. E. Frederick (cofounder of the late Frederick & Nelson department store). (Architect: James J. Chiarelli. Date of Completion: 1962. Original Cost: $1,340,902.) [Costs listed for this and other buildings are considered reasonably close to actual cost at the time of construction, though records of such items are notoriously subject to various interpretations. Identity of funding sources is also often elusive and/or unspecified. The source of money was often the University's General Fund.]

To the east of Memorial Way is the Observatory, a charming little building and the second oldest on campus, built shortly after Denny Hall with the surplus funds and stone from that construction. It still houses its original six-inch clear-aperture telescope, declared at the time to be "the equal of any on the Pacific Coast." The telescope dome rotates on cannon balls left over from the Civil War. On selected clear nights there are free public showings, with slide shows on other evenings. (Architect: Charles W. Saunders. Date of Completion: 1895. Original Cost: $5,000.)

East of the Observatory is the Glenn Hughes Penthouse Theater, originally located on the site of the new Physics/Astronomy Building but relocated to this site in 1992. A performance unit of the School of Drama, the theater was named in memory of Glenn A. Hughes, who joined the faculty in 1919 and continued here until his death in 1964. Its design (by a member of the drama department faculty) was based on the principle of "theater in the round." This mode of performance evolved out of the department's original theatrical experimentations, begun in 1931 and inspired by Professor Hughes's search for a fresh approach to dramatic presentations. At the time of construction it was the first building in the country designed as a theater-in-the-round. Hughes and his students first performed in the penthouse of the Meany Hotel (now Meany Tower), then in other locations; the name Penthouse remained, to be transferred finally to the present building. The theater's

ABOVE LEFT: The Tiffany peacock window
Photo: Stewart Hopkins
ABOVE RIGHT: Burke Museum interior
Photo: Burke Memorial Washington State Museum

EXTERIOR PERSPECTIVE

unique function is expressed by a series of eight glue-laminated roof beams that
define its central interior space. Although admired today, the building's design was
initially (to quote a newspaper article of the day) the "center of a stormy controversy
over its streamlined design amidst solemn Gothic." (Designers: John Ashby Conway
and Glenn Hughes with Carl Gould [his last campus project]. Date of Completion:
1940. Original Cost: $64,328, with both Federal WPA and University funding.)

South of the Penthouse Theater are two buildings serving the School and
Graduate School of Business Administration, planned concurrently but constructed
separately. Built first was MacKenzie Hall, named for Donald H. MacKenzie, formerly chair of the Department of Accounting and a faculty member from 1929 to
1951. It demonstrates the well-intentioned but uncertain early results of freeing campus design from the constraints of collegiate Gothic. In its inner court is the bronze
Fountain of Reflection by George Tsutakawa, a retired UW professor of arts who has
designed a record number of distinctive fountains in this country and abroad. Originally on the grounds of the 1962 Seattle World's Fair, this fountain was later given
to the University by Phi Mu sorority. (Architect: Decker, Christensen and Kitchin.
Date of Completion: 1960. Original Cost: $984,560.)

Balmer Hall, the later of the two, was named for Thomas Balmer, a civic leader
who died in 1959 while a member of the University Board of Regents. Besides classrooms and computing facilities, it also houses the business school's library. Balmer
Hall suffers from much the same design legacy as its partner. A typical example of
the design enthusiasms of the 1960s, it is presently anticipating a major addition and
remodeling with much stronger "contextual" and design ambitions. A 57,000-square-
foot addition to Balmer Hall, designed by Kallmann McKinnell and Wood Architects, is currently under construction. When the addition is completed, Balmer's
gross square footage will exceed 135,600. Until renovation began on Balmer Hall, its
landscape was graced by a Japanese stone lantern, a 1984 gift to the University by
Mr. Mituo Mutai, publisher of the Tokyo newspaper *Yomiuri Shimbun*. (Architects:
Decker & Christensen and Paul Hayden Kirk. Date of Completion: 1962. Original
Cost: $1,702,915.)

Due west of the business school is Denny Hall, the University's first building on its new campus and now the most venerable and honored of its buildings. Originally called the Administration Building, it is on the State Register of Historic Places. Its exterior walls of brick and stone were assembled in an architectural style strongly reminiscent of the early French Renaissance chateaux of the Loire Valley. The architect, Charles W. Saunders, won a competition for the design of the building.

When the cornerstone was laid, the press reported that "the 4th of July, 1894, dawned warm and clear, and by ten o'clock people were already making their way on foot, by trolly and by train to the half-cleared campus . . . ; sheltered from the sun by a temporary stand and umbrellas, about 1000 persons . . ." witnessed ceremonies both celebratory and prolonged. When completed, the building housed the full range of University administration and teaching programs, a 736-seat auditorium, and the library. The steps were for many years adequate to accommodate the full ranks of faculty and students for their annual group picture. (The regents in 1910 renamed the building Denny Hall "in honor especially of Arthur A. Denny, and in honor at the same time of the Denny family.") The original design of the facade included a clock centered over the entrance, but it was not placed there until 1959, a gift of Pi Beta Phi sorority.

The building's crowning feature is a cupola, the work of Gottlieb Weibell, an old-school craftsman. In the cupola hangs Denny Bell, brought around Cape Horn from Troy, New York, in 1862; until 1912, the bell announced classes. First rung by Clarence Bagley (Daniel Bagley's son) when it hung atop the old Territorial University Building, it also pealed for events such as weddings, funerals, and fog warnings, and, most memorably, it signaled the start of the great Seattle fire of 1889. Now mostly silent, it is rung only to announce autumn quarter's homecoming. Brewster Denny, '45, Arthur Denny's great-grandson, is currently at the controls on those occasions. But the cupola nevertheless continues to project the sound of chimes—those of the new digital carillon, latest descendant of the chimes that were lost when their tower burned in 1949. Denny Hall's current occupants are the Departments of Germanics, Anthropology, Classics, and Near Eastern Languages and Literature, and the Language Learning Center.

LEFT: Denny Hall
Photo: Loyd Heath
ABOVE: Denny Yard
Photo: The Seattle Times, *photo archive*

TOP: Denny Hall laboratory, 1897
Photo: University of Washington Libraries, Special Collections and Preservation Division
ABOVE: Denny Hall steps, 1930s
Photo: The Seattle Times, photo archive

Denny Hall's design recalls the many nineteenth-century "Old Mains" on campuses around the country. Threatened with demolition in the mid-1950s, it was saved in 1956 but subjected to rather insensitive interior reconstruction. Today, demolition would be unthinkable, but the building has lost any interior historical character that might have remained from its earlier days. A very recent and thorough exterior cleaning and restoration, however, have returned Denny Hall to its 1895 freshness of color and detail. (Architect: Charles W. Saunders. Date of Completion: 1895. Original Cost: $111,000.)

Denny Hall and the more removed MacKenzie, Raitt, and Savery halls to the east and south give definition to Denny Yard. The earliest "front yard" of the campus, it is one of the open-space features that, along with axes and forms, became established as design principles by the Regents Plan. Because of the scattered and shadowing presence of some monumental freestanding trees, the Yard with its various pedestrian paths is mostly a crisscrossed circulation area. But these mature deciduous and evergreen trees, perhaps remnants of Meany's original "arboretum," lend an august stature to the Yard. Immediately fronting Denny is a splendid black walnut, a native of the eastern United States. The nuts, with their distinctive leathery yellowish-green husks, resist easy harvesting. Just to the south is a grand monkey puzzle tree, a curiosity quite popular in Victorian yards but seldom seen now. An evergreen import from Chile, the tree has branches covered with stiff, sharp, dark green scales that would surely puzzle a monkey or anything else challenged to climb it. King Lane, with its memorial benches, establishes an axial connection from Denny Hall's main entrance southward to Liberal Arts Quad and beyond.

Westward is this sector's last North Campus building, Parrington Hall, another entry on the State Register of Historic Places. Originally called Science Hall, it was maligned by the man for whom it was renamed, Vernon L. Parrington, a University

professor of English for twenty-one years. Much sought-after as a teacher, and a Pulitzer Prize-winner in 1928 for his *Main Currents in American Thought,* Parrington said that the building was "the ugliest I have ever seen." He should have been more generous. The building was originally of unpainted red brick with sandstone trim and had a one-story arched and parapeted front porch (since removed), but the exterior walls were painted shortly after the AYPE, and are now scheduled for further work.

Stylistically, the building is something of an anomaly. If anything, it derives from the Romanesque, with its brick construction and round-headed main entrance and windows. Its classrooms and laboratories initially served the Departments of Geology, Zoology, and Botany, but later construction moved these programs elsewhere. After discussion of possible razing, the regents chose in 1931 to have the building remodeled for the English department, hence its present name. In 1989, it underwent a further extensive interior restoration. Unlike those of Denny Hall, Parrington's restorers approached this rehabilitation with a more understanding hand and a view to enhancing the historical character of the building. It now has the Graduate School of Public Affairs as its principal tenant. (Architect: Josenhans & Allan. Date of Completion: 1902. Original Cost: $66,000. Remodel Architect: Cardwell Thomas. Date of Completion: 1989. Cost: $3,982,943.)

Parrington Hall faces the ninety-foot-high University Flagpole, on axis with Memorial Way, whose vista continues south into Central Plaza. At the pole's base is the Class of 1912 Sundial, of bronze and rough-hewn granite. The dial time varies seasonally up to twenty-three minutes because of Seattle's location two degrees west of the 120th meridian. Don't try to set your watch by it!

Behind Parrington Hall is another of the important campus open spaces, the Campus Green, with its informal clustering of paths, mature trees, and lawns. This

TOP: Denny Hall
Photo: Chris Eden/Eden Arts
ABOVE: Campus Green
Photo: Barry Provorse

parklike amenity opens both to the campus and to Northeast Forty-second Street and the University District. (In the troubled campus atmosphere of the late 1960s and early 1970s, the Green was inelegantly known as Hippie Hill.) The regularity of some of its tree plantings suggests that here, again, may be reminders of Meany's ambitions for a campus arboretum. In the southwest corner of the Green is Madrona Grove, whose gradual decline the University is attempting to correct.

North across Fifteenth Avenue Northeast at the corner of Northeast Forty-fifth Street is the R. Bronsdon "Curly" Harris Alumni House, an elegant and sophisticated building that was originally the Baptist Student Center, but was acquired in 1977 by the University Alumni Association. Its namesake was from 1936 to 1964 the association's executive director, an enthusiastic and successful supporter of University and association interests. (Architect: Roland Terry. Date of Completion: 1963. Original Cost: unknown.)

At the far northwest corner of the campus, enclosed by a protective belt of trees and plantings, is the largest North Campus parking lot. It is worth mentioning only because the area had been designated for future student dormitories in the Regents Plan. But by 1935 the University had changed its mind and moved those sites eastward to the northeast sector, thus insulating its students further from the seductions of "the Ave" (University Way Northeast), the popular shopping, eating, and gathering strip that parallels the campus one block to the west. Instead, this area was preserved as an informal expanse of woods and paths. But the 1950s, with their automotive priorities, saw clearance for parking on both sides of Memorial Way, prompting one wry professorial remark that the campus was now "the nation's only parking lot with a university on it!"

Northeast Sector

This corner of the campus was originally assigned to the University's athletic program and was the location of its first gymnasium. It was here that the 1896 gymnasium had been built, with a playing field to the south, now Denny Field, behind Hutchinson Hall. The scene of some of the University's early football successes, the field was fenced and provided with wood-frame covered bleachers on both its north and south sides. But with the 1935 decision to relocate dormitories from the north-

TOP: Parrington Hall, originally named Science Hall, was completed in 1902 at a cost of $66,000. *Photo: University of Washington Libraries, Special Collections and Preservation Division*
ABOVE: Parrington Hall, biology laboratory *Photo: University of Washington Libraries, Special Collections and Preservation Division*

west corner of campus to the northeast, the area was given the assignment that dominates it today. Denny Field, however, still remains a playfield, along with its fringes of tennis courts.

The first of the University's modern dorms (and the first built since construction of Lewis and Clark halls in 1899) is today's Hansee Hall. Located just off Northeast Forty-fifth Street and east of Klickitat Lane, in one of the most environmentally romantic sites on campus, Hansee is a complex of collegiate-Gothic gabled roofs, arched doorways, oriel windows, chimneys, cupola, patterned brick, and gardened courtyards. The courtyards are formed by the four separate wings of the building (designed originally for 325 women), altogether an ensemble that comes close to the elegant Ivy League residence halls by which it was so clearly inspired. Each wing has a separate "house" designation carrying the name of a woman important in state and University history: Eliza Ferry Leary, daughter of the first governor of the state of Washington; Catherine V. Blaine, Seattle's first schoolteacher; Ruth Karr McKee, first woman appointed to the Board of Regents; and Isabella Austin, appointed dean of women in 1909. In 1961, the regents gave the building the cumulative name of Hansee Hall, honoring Martha Lois Hansee, a turn-of-the-century dean of women. During the Second World War, Hansee was a barracks for the Naval ROTC and Marine officer candidates. Note in the east court a magnificent tulip poplar, a native easterner adding its presence to the romance. (Architects: David J. Myers and John Graham. Date of Completion: 1936. Original Cost: $630,000, a combination of Federal [WPA] and state [SERF] emergency funds.)

Hansee Hall
Photo: Stewart Hopkins

Haggett Hall entry
Photo: Stewart Hopkins

One of the most pleasant paths on campus runs eastward south of Hansee Hall to the campus ridge, which still has remnants of its wooded past overlooking the flatlands beyond Montlake Boulevard. Here along Whitman Court is a sequence of postwar dormitories whose designs reflect the changing policies of the University toward its students and its responsibilities in loco parentis. (The original single-sex dorms have evolved into a coeducational system.)

The most northerly of the group, McCarty Hall, was named in memory of Clara McCarty, who received the University's first degree in 1876. Designed as a dorm for six hundred women and built in two phases, it is fully modernist in style, making no architectural gesture toward its collegiate-Gothic neighbor to the west but responding adroitly to the demanding topography of its site. (Architect: Young, Richardson and Carleton. Dates of Completion: 1960, 1962. Original Cost: $1,946,327, $1,069,055.)

South of McCarty Hall is a dramatically different dormitory, Haggett Hall, whose double and coeducational towers honor two Haggetts—Professor Arthur Haggett, who came to the University in 1917 as a professor of Greek and later became dean of the College of Liberal Arts; and his wife, Winifred S. Haggett, dean of women from 1923 to 1939. The original assignment by the University was one tower for women, the other for men, with an eight-hundred-student capacity. Single-sex housing was maintained, but the University permitted the sharing of lounge and dining facilities in the foundation structure from which the two towers rise. It was a compromise policy, edging toward giving students more responsibility for their conduct. The towers, with their angled window bays, are oriented toward the view but seem designed to suggest that visual exchange between the sexes ought to be

ABOVE: Haggett Hall, an eight-hundred-student
dormitory, was completed in 1963.
Photo: Stewart Hopkins
OVERLEAF: Cascade Mountains at dawn from
McMahon Hall
Photo: Stewart Hopkins

discouraged! As another index of the times, parking is provided for 166 cars. (Architect: Kirk, Wallace, McKinley & Associates. Date of Completion: 1963. Original Cost: $4,256,603.)

McMahon Hall, to the south, is the last of the campus east-ridge dorms. A coed dorm from its beginnings, this one houses eleven hundred students. The building's complex and brutalist form of reinforced concrete places its students in suites of five or six rooms clustered about a shared common area rather than in conventional rows of single rooms. Assignment of each suite to either all men or women is the only remnant of the University's past role in loco parentis. Here is another dorm whose name does double duty. Edward McMahon was a professor of history from 1908 to 1940 and sometime departmental chairman; his wife, Theresa McMahon, was a teacher of economics and business from 1911 to 1937. Much of McMahon Hall's visual interest comes from the intricacies of its framing pattern and living room balconies. Its lower levels have parking for 180 cars. (Architect: Kirk, Wallace, McKinley & Associates. Date of Completion: 1965. Original Cost: $6,607,800.)

Northward from McMahon Hall on Stevens Way (the principal circumferential circulation route of the campus) is Lewis Hall, a venerable brick remnant of earliest campus history. Named for the famous explorer Meriwether Lewis, it was built originally as a fifty-student men's dorm. For reasons uncertain it became Pierrepont Hall in 1903 and served as a display building during the AYPE. Renamed Lewis Hall in 1917, it became a women's dorm after the war. Lewis was completely rebuilt with

LEFT: McMahon Hall, an eleven-hundred-student dormitory, was completed in 1965 at a cost of $6.6 million.
Photo: Stewart Hopkins
ABOVE: Hutchinson Hall was, until 1984, the women's physical education building.
Photo: Stewart Hopkins

WPA labor in 1936 and became the School of Communications. Today it gives shelter to a miscellaneous collection of administrative and doctoral-student offices, but any interior design details have been thoroughly sanitized by successive remodelings over the years. (Architect: Josenhans & Allan. Date of Completion: 1899. Original Cost: $25,000.)

Farther up Stevens Way is Hutchinson Hall, built originally as the women's physical education building, a replacement for the old gymnasium that had since 1896 occupied a nearby site to the north. Named in 1941 to honor Mary G. Hutchinson and her years at the University (1919 to 1947), including eleven years as an executive officer in the physical education department, it continues to carry her name, although it now houses the School of Drama and its library. Hutchinson Hall's gothicized horizontal form and substantial entry tower with its Gothic traceried window make interesting contributions to the campus design features along Stevens Way. (Architect: Bebb and Gould. Date of Completion: 1927. Original Cost: $312,038.)

North Campus holds many of the University's built-environment roots, its oldest buildings: Denny, Parrington, and Lewis halls, and the Observatory. Many of the University's most venerable open spaces are here as well, including Denny Yard, the Campus Green, and Denny Field. This is where it all began.

LEFT: Lewis Hall, shown here in 1995, was built as the men's dormitory in 1899 for $25,000.
Photo: Stewart Hopkins
RIGHT: Campus fall colors
Photo: Loyd Heath

CHAPTER SEVEN

Central Campus

CENTRAL CAMPUS IS THE MOST ARCHITECTURALLY AND GEOGRAPHICALLY
diverse area of the University. It includes the collegiate-Gothic Liberal Arts Quadrangle and examples of modernism, including the third addition to Suzzallo Library and Sieg Hall; brutalism, represented by Condon, Schmitz, and Gould halls; and contextualism, the most recent campus architectural idiom, which guided the designs of Allen Library, the Physics/Astronomy Building, and the new Chemistry Building. It extends from the flat, tree-lined Campus Parkway across campus, ending at the Center for Urban Horticulture on the University's eastern border. Because of its natural and built environmental variety, Central Campus is perhaps the most interesting area within the University's boundaries.

Liberal Arts Quadrangle

Of campus spaces, none is more hallowed than Liberal Arts Quadrangle. The unity of the quad's architectural framework in building heights, materials, and details (almost entirely the work of the architects Bebb and Gould) makes this the universal campus favorite of its genre. The landscape treatment deserves much of the credit: the simplicity of its floor of lawns and bricked walks and the ranks of Yoshino cherry trees that parallel its walls admirably reinforce the rectilinear clarity of the quad's plan. The trees, originally in the arboretum south of the Museum of History and Industry, were scheduled to be destroyed to make way for approaches to the Evergreen Point Bridge. President Odegaard made the inspired decision to move them to the quad in 1964. Cherry blossom time here is a celebratory event!

Enclosure of the quad began in 1916 with construction of Raitt Hall (originally the Home Economics Building), in large part at the initiative of the director of the School of Home Economics, Effie Isobel Raitt. She began her career in 1912 at the University, teaching first in Denny Hall and later in a leaky temporary wartime shack north of Denny. Despite a shy personality, she combined ambition and determination to successfully lobby the legislators. "Nor was she above a bit of gentle guile," says the University publication *A Campus Walk:*

> She invited legislators to a luncheon in the shack and, as luck would
> have it, it was a rainy day. The roof leaked steadily, lunch was soggy, and
> a few days later the legislature of 1915 appropriated funds for a new struc-
> ture for home economics.

Until the early 1960s, Raitt Hall's ground floor held the Commons, a cafeteria-type campus facility. This was well before the present extensive and coordinated campus food-services program had been developed. Ironically, some years ago, with the University in the throes of budget cutting, and in light of changing academic priorities, the home economics department was closed. Today the building is quarters for nutritional sciences and the Department of Speech Communications.

Suzzallo Library, Graduate Reading Room,
renamed Suzzallo Reading Room in 1991
Photo: Stewart Hopkins

95

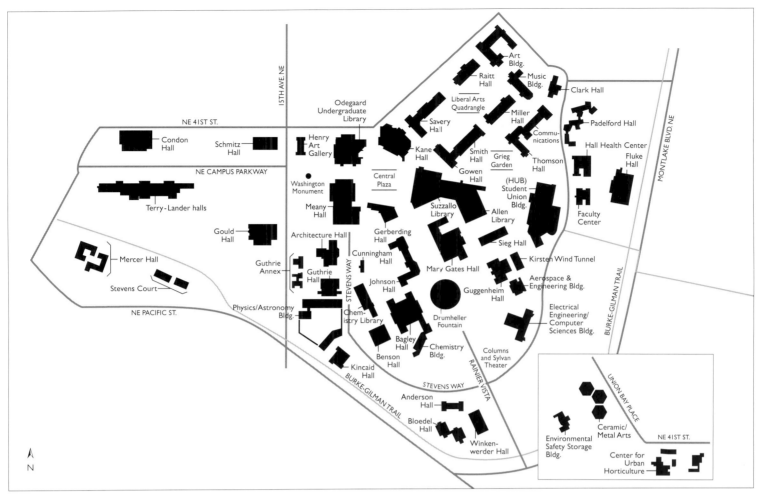

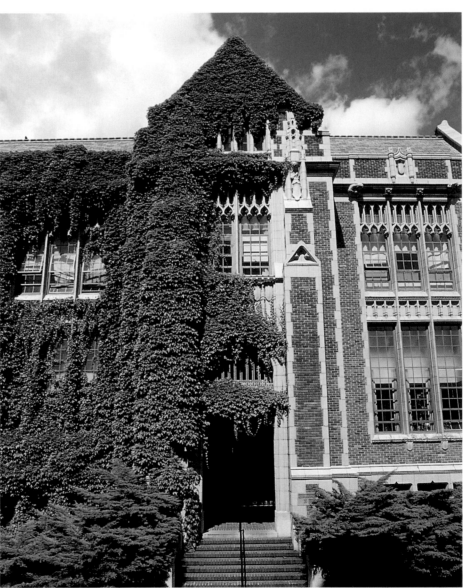

ABOVE: Central Campus map
RIGHT: The climbing vines of Miller Hall
Photo: Barry Provorse

Raitt Hall was the first product of the new design policy dictating collegiate Gothic for upper campus buildings—and the first of Carl Gould's interpretations of that policy. The building's palette of materials and colors endured for use in similar work elsewhere on campus. Gould also called for decoration that would charm the eye and, in this case, reflect the building's function—though by today's standards his choices would be politically incorrect. Along the cornice line is a series of figures, designed by Gould, of women making bread, carding wool, sewing, scrubbing clothes, and gathering fruits and vegetables. There is a single male figure (like a bearded Gould) shown Moses-like holding a tablet relief plan of Liberal Arts Quad (though some have interpreted it as the man "laying down the law"). Both Gould and Suzzallo had firm ideas about the policy on decorative gargoyles for the quad's buildings. Lillian Brown Getty, Suzzallo's secretary, recalled that "Dr. Suzzallo had more or less difficulty with Carl Gould, the architect, regarding these gargoyles. Gould wanted them to resemble living people and H.S. [sic] insisted they be symbolic. . . . Dr. Suzzallo used to say, 'I have to keep Carl straight in these matters.'" (Architect: Bebb and Gould. Date of Completion: 1916. Original Cost: $151,292.)

Quad development next turned due west from Raitt Hall to Commerce Hall, followed shortly thereafter by Philosophy Hall, which together formed an ell in plan and established the quad's southwest corner. The legislature approved a program whereby the Commerce Hall construction was funded through student payments into the University's building fund, thereby making this the first of the state's institutions of higher education to require tuition. From 1958 to 1972, Philosophy Hall carried the name Guthrie Hall, but since 1972 the two buildings have shared their common identity as Savery Hall, named in 1947 for William Savery, who headed the Department of Philosophy from his arrival on campus in 1902 until his death in 1945. In addition to that department and its library, Savery Hall shelters the Departments of Economics and Sociology.

Following the model established by Raitt Hall in form and materials, Savery Hall also includes cornice sculptures, these by Alonzo Victor Lewis, but with no special reference to the building's occupants. One can discover representations of a miscellany of activities—occupational, academic, even sporting, including crew, tennis, and track. A postwar reminiscence of World War I is the sculptured presence in the cornice of General Pershing. (Architect: Bebb and Gould for both Commerce and Philosophy halls. Date of Completion: Commerce Hall, 1917; Philosophy Hall (interrupted by the war), 1920. Original Cost: Commerce Hall, $203,404; Philosophy Hall, $388,121.)

In the 1920s, construction turned to the quad's northeast corner with completion of Education Hall, now known as Miller Hall, in honor of the record and power as regent of William Winlock Miller, whose length of tenure (1913–1957) remains unmatched. As chair of the regents' Building and Grounds Committee, he maintained the upper campus collegiate-Gothic standards.

Miller Hall was once the seat of the President's office, the registrar, and like administrative functions, as well as the Colleges of Education and Engineering and the sculpture and architecture programs. Today it has a single occupant, the College of Education. Sculptor Alonzo Lewis created a versatile mix of figures for the building's artful cornices, including professors, students, men in top hats, a woman at the harp, an aged Chinese, and Mercury! In autumn the Virginia creeper covering Miller's walls turns to fiery shades of red, orange, and yellow. (Architect: Bebb and Gould. Date of Completion: 1922. Original Cost: $453,000.)

At the building's southwest corner is a Spanish fir, one of the few true firs on the campus, noted for its dark green needles and the five-inch-long "candles" of its

ABOVE: Commerce and Philosophy halls became Savery Hall in 1972.
Photo: Mary Levin, University of Washington, News and Information
OVERLEAF, FROM LEFT: Miller Hall, Smith Hall, and Gowen Hall
Photo: Stewart Hopkins

cones. Skagit Lane, which parallels the southeast facade of the quad, is lined with horse chestnuts that flower handsomely in the spring and scatter yellow leaves and mahogany-colored nuts with spiked husks on the ground in the fall.

Next, back to the west end of the quad, came the construction of Condon Hall, since renamed Gowen Hall. The first work on the quad by an architect other than Bebb and Gould, it nevertheless follows closely the already well-established design precedents. Specifically designed to house the School of Law, the building features handsome wood-paneled interiors behind its collegiate-Gothic walls. The building's current name dates from 1972, when law was preparing to move unhappily to its new quarters elsewhere. Gowen now is occupied by the Departments of Asian Languages and Literature (and its library) and Political Science.

The renaming as Gowen Hall recalls the long career on campus of Herbert H. Gowen. An Episcopal minister who from 1909 to 1944 was a professor of Oriental studies (often the only one), Gowen taught courses on Chinese, Japanese, Indian, and Near Eastern literature and history, as well as the history of religion and Hebrew, Arabic, and Sanskrit. At the same time, he was a familiar figure in many of Seattle's Episcopal pulpits. *A Campus Walk* notes that Gowen was alleged to have read a book a day.

> Scores of former University students and faculty members remember seeing him stroll across the campus, head down as he read one of the thousands of volumes he consumed during his lifetime, pockets sagging with the weight of still more books yet to be read. Gowen continued his learning habits until the day of his death in 1960 at the age of 96.

Gowen Hall's exterior is rich in iconography, though that of its former occupant rather than its present ones. Featured on its west facade are sculptured medallions by John Elliot of Hammurabi, Solon, Moses, and other great historical law givers. (Architect: A. H. Albertson. Date of Completion: 1932. Original Cost: $376,565.)

The final Liberal Arts Quad construction phase before the coming of the Second World War was Smith Hall, built as home base for the Departments of History and Geography (and the geography library). Originally Social Science Hall, it was renamed to honor James Allen Smith, who as a professor of political science from 1897 to 1924 (eleven of those years as dean of the Graduate School) established another of the University's venerable campus reputations. Though the building's design lacks some of the richness of its quad neighbors, it does have picturesque contributions to make in the twenty-eight figures sculptured for it by Dudley Pratt, who was on the art faculty at the time. *A Campus Walk* catalogues the figures:

> At the east end are six sculptures symbolizing basic human needs and emotions: family, love, shelter, food, rest, and laughter. At the southeast corner are figures depicting the primitive concept of weather.
>
> And on the northeast corner are a Buddha-like gargoyle signifying the knowledge of the Orient, a book-laden "egghead" representing the intelligent democracy of America, a World War I soldier in a gasmask as the power of Europe, and a bongo drummer representing the magic of Africa. Of unusual interest are the two groups on the north side portraying Seattle's early history and Seattle in 1939, the year the building was constructed. Among the former are Indians, a totem, a fish, and a cougar. In the latter group are sculptural grotesques of a logger, a construction worker, a trucker, and an engineer clutching what appears to be a slide rule.

The Art Building was completed in 1949 and, with the Music Building, closed the northeast end of the quad.
Photo: Chris Eden/Eden Arts

At the northeast end of the building, entry stairs lead past a wall-mounted terra-cotta model of the Regents Plan for the campus. (Architect: Bebb and Gould. Date of Completion: 1939. Original Cost: $1,600,000.)

At the northeast corner of Smith Hall, by Skagit Lane, stands what is known as the Edmond S. Meany sequoia, a giant tree whose stature justifies its name. Meany, long committed to having an arboretum on the campus, was active in its landscaping, even using his own garden for the nurturing of seedlings from many parts of the country for eventual campus planting by him and his students. This sequoia is one of "Meany's trees" that still remains to remind us of his efforts.

Work on the quad resumed following the end of the war. Beginning the closure of the northeast end was the Art Building in 1949, followed the next year by the Music Building, respectively housing the School of Art and its offices, classrooms, studios, and library, and the School of Music, with similar facilities. Together, they now complete the quad ensemble, providing form and a pair of belfries that establish the easterly gateway for a vista that, alas, leads nowhere. The Regents Plan—and those that followed—anticipated that there would be some sort of closure to that framed axis, preferably a prominent building. But the most recent General Physical Development Plan fails to restate for the future this rather elemental space-planning principle, offering only a noncommittal vacuum in a place given considerable prominence by its relationship to the campus design framework.

These two buildings, both products of upper-campus collegiate-Gothic controls, are, under the circumstances, appropriate for their assigned role in the quad design

context. Twins, but not identical (including the Art Building's later substantial eastward addition), each has a single tenant. The Art Building houses the Jacob Lawrence Gallery, which features displays of student work and is open to the public. (Architect: Art Building and Music Building, Whitehouse & Price; 1969 Art Building addition, Alfred H. Croonquist. Date of Completion: Art Building, 1949 and 1969; Music Building, 1950. Original Cost: Art Building, $1,263,387; Music Building, $1,684,610.)

At the Art Building's south corner in the quad is a magnificent purple beech, whose color in full leaf has a wonderful foil in the brick wall just behind it. North of the building, between it and Stevens Way, are two English hollies known as George and Martha Washington, in reference to the Mount Vernon hollies from which the seeds were propagated; Francis J. Turnball gave the hollies to the University in 1930.

Central Plaza

Halfway down the length of Liberal Arts Quad is King Lane, leading northward to Denny Yard and Denny Hall and southward toward the HUB, the Student Union Building. Across and at right angles to it is the quad's long axis, which sweeps so inconclusively to the northeast but in its reverse direction binds this quad dramatically with Central Plaza (called Central Quadrangle in early planning documents and Red Square in present-day parlance) to the southwest. Part One of this book recounts the status the plaza enjoyed in the successive plans that featured it, beginning with its earliest realization as the Court of Honor before the U.S. Government Building at the AYPE. As now seen, the plaza is of rather recent origin, the design with the 1,000-car garage beneath it coming primarily from the cooperative efforts of two architectural firms.

Work began on the plaza in the late 1960s during a time of considerable campus unrest, which introduced further controversy into an already contentious project. Student protests centered on the "irrelevance" of building a garage amidst the ongoing Vietnam War, as well as on concerns over social turmoil, political issues, and even the disappearance of the paths and open lawn that had given the space its previous inviting informality.

But in 1971 Central Plaza became a reality. Its brick paving and austerity make it the most urbane of the campus open spaces, but its efforts to extend a more humanistic welcome to visitors have generally failed. Among these efforts are the six substantial trees along the north side of the Administration Building, northern red oaks that thrive because they are planted in ground outside the walls of the underground garage. Their much more spindly crab-apple companions paralleling Meany Hall to the west (replacements for earlier trees that failed) are disadvantaged by being planted in containers suspended within the perimeter of the garage. One humanizing element in the plaza that does succeed is the line of steps before Kane Hall. On sunny days this is a favorite sitting spot, where students make a willing audience for street performers and speakers of assorted political/religious persuasions.

The plaza's paving pattern is reminiscent of medieval European town squares, especially the Piazza del Campo in Siena. During design stages there had been some talk about using grass rather than paving, but that approach was discouraged by the likelihood of all sorts of spontaneous path patterns responding to the quad's multiple entries and by the prospect of heavy, rain-sodden lawns above the garage. The abstract geometry of the trio of brick pylons brings a certain grandeur to the plaza, their location calculated to harmonize well with the surrounding partnership of buildings and Memorial Way. In effect, they become a kind of University campanile

LEFT: With the opening of the Music Building in 1950, Gould's ambitious master plan for Liberal Arts Quadrangle was complete.
Photo: Stewart Hopkins
OVERLEAF: Central Plaza
Photo: Chris Eden/Eden Arts

(lacking only the bells), though their true function as vents for the garage below diminishes their status as monument.

On the other hand, Barnett Newman's *Broken Obelisk* does provide a much-needed embellishment to the plaza. Noted mainly as an abstract color field painter, Newman created two other versions of the Cor-Ten steel obelisk—one for Houston, Texas, the other in New York City at the Museum of Modern Art. Interestingly, the podium on which it rests was a part of the original plaza plan, located so that a future sculpture placed there would complement its neighbor, Kane Hall, and work well within the plaza, establishing a relationship with the axis and connecting vista that reaches out of Central Plaza toward Liberal Arts Quad, and vice versa. Thus, when the Virginia Wright Foundation offered the twenty-six-foot-high steel obelisk to the University in 1971, the sculpture proved to be inspired in design, placement, and timing.

The centrality of the plaza makes it the focus of other axes; one leads westward along Campus Parkway to the distant Olympics, a window both out of and into the campus. On line with this vista is the bronze George Washington Monument, a Larado Taft work that was purchased in 1909 through contributions of the Daughters of the American Revolution, schoolchildren from around the state, and a leg-

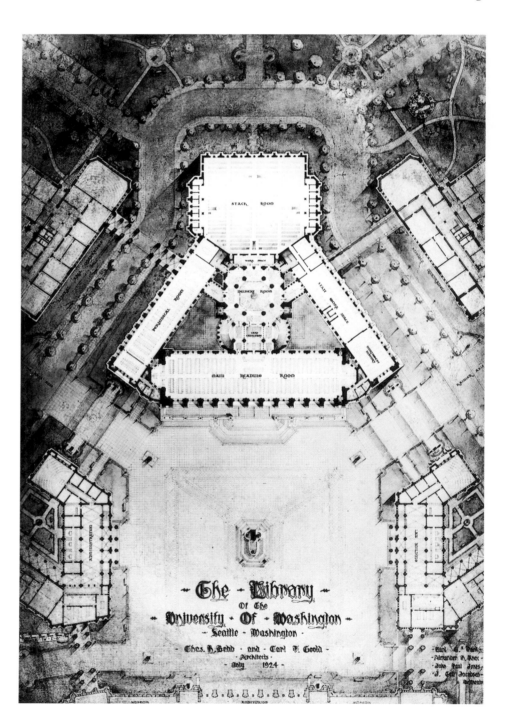

The Bebb and Gould plan for the University's library (which became Suzzallo Library in 1933), administration and law buildings, and what became Central Plaza
Photo: University of Washington Libraries, Special Collections and Preservation Division

islative appropriation. It was featured at the Northeast Forty-first Street entrance to the AYPE before being placed in its present location on February 22, 1939, on axis with the later Campus Parkway. There is also the axis dividing Kane Hall from the Odegaard Library, where, looking north, one sees the flagpole that marks the southern end of Memorial Way. But the principal axis thrusting out from the plaza, the one that was the heart of the AYPE plan and continues in that role for the University, is Rainier Vista, that superb example of what the Japanese call *shakkei,* borrowed scenery. The borrowee is in this case Mount Rainier! (Plaza Architects: Kirk, Wallace, McKinley & Associates; Walker and McGough. Date of Completion: 1971. Original Cost: $608,000.)

Suzzallo Library

The architecture that frames Central Plaza spans almost fifty years, beginning in 1926 with Suzzallo Library, named for the University's fifteenth president, Henry Suzzallo, and ending with the new Meany Hall in 1974. It is appropriate, given President Suzzallo's feelings about the library and its place in University life, that it should lead the parade of developments on the quad. In 1921, the University's main library was still housed in the wood-frame, flammable, and "temporary" Washington State Pavilion, which was left over from the AYPE; seating capacity was 300 for a University student population of 6,631. A new library was not only a pressing need but also a project close to President Suzzallo's heart.

The regents agreed, and on April 2, 1922, they authorized Bebb and Gould to prepare plans for the new building. The plans that emerged were for long-range construction over a period of years and successive budgets, an equilateral triangle enclosing a space out of which would rise a towering campanile. In size, height, and placement, the library would visually dominate the central quadrangle and reaffirm in physical terms its function in the intellectual life of the University. What Gould developed would become the most ambitious essay in the University's panoply of collegiate Gothic. It was intended, he said, "to be for all time the outstanding and dominating feature on the campus." The first phase of construction was the wing that faced west, defining the east edge of the central quad and looking toward Meany Hall; ground was broken on April 3, 1923.

Suzzallo Library stairs
Photo: Mary Levin, University of Washington, News and Information

The dominant feature of the library's west facade (brick, terra-cotta, and cast stone) is the row of eleven great thirty-five-foot-high Gothic-traceried stained-glass windows, expressing the soaring heights of the vaulted Suzzallo Reading Room, which runs the full length of the second floor. They are separated by piers that reach from the building's entrance terrace to pinnacles above the roof parapet to establish the rhythm of the Gothic structure (though without any Gothic structural principles; what you see both externally and internally is a romantic envelope enclosing a modern steel-frame structural skeleton).

The iconography of the library is especially rich, appropriate given the ambitions all seemed to have for it. The Board of Regents' report for 1925 credits Seattle businessman Horace C. Henry (whose interest in the University had been cultivated by Suzzallo) with a $4,800 contribution to "enable the University to construct a library building adorned with sculptured figures that shall be a continual source of inspiration to all persons. . . ." The results are apparent in the number of sculptures on the building. Tacoma sculptor Alan Clark's three cast-stone figures are featured at the main entrance: a bearded old man, *Thought;* a young woman, *Inspiration;* and a poised and alert young man, *Mastery.* In the belt course just above the first-floor windows are incised in gothicized lettering the names of the academic disciplines: Philosophy, Religion, Jurisprudence, Medicine, Letters and Science, Technology, and Fine Arts. At the lower level of the piers, between the reading-room windows, are

shields of other universities. Above them are eighteen niches holding four-and-a-half-foot terra-cotta figures of major contributors to learning and culture. From left to right: Moses, Pasteur, Dante, Shakespeare, Plato, Franklin (the only American), Justinian, Newton, da Vinci, Galileo, Goethe, Herodotus, Adam Smith, Homer, Gutenberg, Beethoven, Darwin, and Grotius. These 18 men were selected by faculty members from 246 nominations. One wonders what their choices might be today.

Above the doors in ironwork are the names and dates of the earliest printers: Tao Feng, Gutenberg, Caxton, Aldus, Estienne, and El Zevier. Upon entering, visitors see on the wall ahead *The Waiting Multitude,* by local sculptor and UW alumnus Ray Jensen. On both right and left, the sweeping curves of stairs to the second-floor rotunda lead past the sheet-steel sculpture *Circum Okto,* by Jon Geise of Seattle, and on to the Suzzallo Reading Room, the most spectacular interior space on campus, and possibly one of the most monumental built spaces in the state (along with the domed state capitol rotunda in Olympia). The cathedral-like room is 241 feet long, 52 feet across, and 65 feet high; its high windows carry in their insert designs medallions of the watermarks used by early printers, as well as other decorative devices developed by the architects, based on suggestions from Charles W. Smith, the University reference librarian of those days.

Many of the room's long oak tables and chairs were designed by the architects, as were the fine oak friezes above the bookshelves with their carvings of native Washington fruits, flowers, and shrubs (rhododendron, dogwood, Douglas fir, trillium, salmonberry, wild rose). All were the work of H. L. Erickson. Elaborate iron and glass light fixtures in a double row accent the sequence of piers supporting the ceiling, carrying the designs and colors worked out by Gould. Large decorative world globes hang in the apses at either end of the room. Following some years of unsympathetic use for study carrels and storage, the room has recently been handsomely restored to its rightful place as the jewel in the library's crown.

In 1935, construction was completed on the south-facing second side of the library's original equilateral plan, providing a variety of administrative and specialized support areas. Architecturally, its collegiate Gothic blends seamlessly with the first phase of the building. Especially notable is the Smith Room (named for the aforementioned Charles W. Smith, who eventually became University librarian in his forty-two years of University service, 1905 to 1947). Located at the west end of the new wing, the room has a rich inventory of iconography, commensurate with what Gould established in the original wing. Most of this is found in the designs of the Gothic-traceried windows, with their many medallions and other inserts having regional and historical references.

When it came time for the library's third-phase construction, circumstances had changed. The era was the 1960s, a period of design that was free of collegiate-Gothic restraints but still uncertain as to how best to guide and use its new design initiatives. The format of the equilateral triangle, established for the library in the Regents Plan, was abandoned, in part the victim of library needs far exceeding the space limits imposed by the earlier plan. Those needs, plus new and austere design goals, resulted in a building that seemed supportable then but that time and changing expectations have largely discredited. Nevertheless, the new wing at least enabled the library to contend with its explosive expansion for the next quarter century.

The Allen Library, though essentially a fourth-phase expansion of Suzzallo, is the latest wing, named in honor of Kenneth S. Allen. A member of the library's staff from 1951 and its associate director from 1960 until his death in 1982, he was the father of Paul G. Allen, cofounder of Microsoft, Inc., whose gifts for the library totaled more than $12 million, $2 million of which helped finance the new wing. The design responds to contemporary concerns about existing architectural and campus

ABOVE: Grant Lane
Photo: Stewart Hopkins
RIGHT: The Smith Wing, the second side of the Bebb and Gould plan for the University's library
Photo: Chris Eden/Eden Arts

Allen Library
Photo: Stewart Hopkins

context; its form, scale, massing, texture, details, and materials are chosen in recognition of its neighbors and the design relationships they represent. Made of some four hundred thousand bricks in four colors and five patterns, Allen's patterned walls echo similar surfaces on nearby buildings of the 1930s. Energy conservation, a more recent preoccupation, is also addressed here in the use of insulating glass, whose light-green tint provides protection from the sun and control of ultraviolet rays. At the time of its construction, Allen was the University's single most costly building. It also makes an important space-design contribution to the campus: its arcade responds to a major cross-campus circulation route and acts as a dramatic entry point into or out of the HUB Yard. The building itself brings definition to the yard and the east campus area.

Specialized facilities are now provided by Allen for the Natural Sciences Library, Special Collections and Preservation, Manuscripts and University Archivist, and libraries administration, as well as additional space for the collections and their users. Allen and Suzzallo together provide a total of sixty miles of shelving. With a collection exceeding five million volumes, University libraries are among the top fifteen research libraries in the nation. (Architects: Phase 1, Bebb and Gould; Phase 2, Bebb and Jones; Phase 3, Bindon and Wright; Phase 4 [Allen Library], Edward Larrabee Barnes/John M. Y. Lee & Partners. Date of Completion: 1926, 1935, 1963, 1991. Original Cost: Phase 1, $894,000; Phase 2, $476,144; Phase 3, $4,666,450; Phase 4, $23,000,000 for building and HUB Yard renovation, $38,000,000 for total project.)

The Administration Building was the next to be developed of Central Plaza's framing structures. The first major structure erected after World War II, built entirely of cast stone, it is the most pretentious example of collegiate Gothic on campus. All the characteristic motifs of the genre, including towers, pointed arches, gabled roofs, pinnacles, sculptured bosses, and gargoyles, are found there. Along the parapets are twenty-five sculptures, Dudley Pratt's last work for the University. They depict the various academic disciplines, including fisheries and oceanography, embodied by Father Neptune on the building's east gable. Each face of the seventy-foot tower (housing a stairway, not bells, though early plans suggested a belfry there) features Phi Beta Kappa keys as part of its liberal arts decoration. Above the tower door is a shield in relief featuring a profile of Herbert T. Condon, a "Friend of Youth" whose years of devotion to the University culminated in his serving as dean of students from 1940 to 1949. He retired in 1951.

At the other end of the building facing the plaza is a more informal memorial relief: a Husky supporting a UW shield. Between the windows of the first and second floors are spandrels repeating in bronze the seals of Washington Territory, the University, and the state of Washington. Above the entry porch on the south side is an academically gowned male figure holding a money bag in one hand and an adding machine in the other. The building continues to house the key University administrative offices, including those of the President and the Board of Regents, as well as the office of the Graduate School. In 1995 the Administration Building was renamed William P. Gerberding Hall to honor the retiring president. (Architects: Victor N. Jones and John T. Jacobsen. Date of Completion: 1949. Original Cost: $1,561,924.)

Construction activity around the future Central Plaza was suspended for over twenty years after completion of the Administration Building. One frustrating barrier was the presence of old Meany Hall, a holdover from the AYPE, useful enough but awkwardly located within the plans that had evolved for the area's future. However, a major blip on this otherwise quiet screen was the earthquake of 1965, which so damaged Meany Hall that it was condemned and shortly thereafter pulled down. Nature had now cleared the field for further definitive action, which came in a crescendo of construction in the first part of the 1970s. First to move ahead was Kane Hall, named for the University's somewhat ill-starred fourteenth president, the scholarly Thomas F. Kane. First named acting president in 1902, Kane was later given a permanent appointment. Although his tenure was a period of great growth in student numbers (from 650 to 2,824), he failed to win the confidence of the regents, who were looking for a kind of leadership more in tune with their growing expectations for the University's future. The defiant Kane was ultimately forced to resign, clearing the way for the coming of President Suzzallo.

Kane Hall has a frankly brutal presence on the plaza. Its heavy concrete piers, opening to the plaza, evoke visions in their scale and structure of a hydroelectric dam's penstocks; only the water is missing. The rhythm of the piers does suggest a consciousness of the similar structural module in Suzzallo Library, to the east. Kane Hall was designed to house a group of large classrooms and the Roethke Auditorium, the latter named for the Pulitzer Prize–winning poet Theodore Roethke, who was at the University from 1947 until his death in 1963. The large second-floor windows opening out to the plaza belong to the handsome Walker Ames Room, a kind of University reception hall where various ceremonial and special events are commodiously held. The room is named for the Walker Ames family, which gave generously to the University, including the 1907 Madison Park house used as the University president's home. In the room is a charming musical cynosure, the Littlefield Organ, which was dedicated in 1990. Its carved wood case is a wonderfully rich foil to the room's understated elegance.

Grant Lane and Allen Library
Photo: Mary Levin, University of Washington, News and Information

Also on the second floor of Kane is the lobby, with its large, irregularly shaped *Shipscalers' Mural,* painted in 1945 by Pablo O'Higgins for the local union hall of the Shipscalers, Drydock, and Boatworkers Union. When the hall was sold and later torn down, the mural was donated to the University. A suitable place for rehanging was not found, so it was stored and then inexplicably forgotten. Rediscovered in 1975, the mural was given this new and appropriate setting. (Architect: Walker, McGough, Foltz, Lyerla. Date of Completion: 1971. Original Cost: $4,414,777.)

Just west of Kane is Odegaard Undergraduate Library, so named at the time of President Charles Odegaard's retirement in 1973. Inside the library, on the second floor, is a bronze bust of Odegaard by Everett DuPen of the School of Art. This was a retirement gift to Odegaard from the University's Alumni Association and the Board of Regents. The library also has a handsome portrait of Odegaard by Seattle artist Ted Rand. The three-story library's interior surrounds a monumental staircase and atrium that open visually to all the library floors and book collections. There are also fully equipped audio-visual study cubicles, whose expression on the exterior of this concrete-frame and brick building makes for an interesting visual presence on the plaza. The lower floor houses By George, one of the units in the University's food-services chain. When this building was being planned, the librarians were adamant that there be no food odors seeping up into their library; as a

result there is no direct connection between the library interior and its lower-level partner. There is, however, a direct connection between the library and the plaza garage. (Architect: Kirk, Wallace, McKinley & Associates. Date of Completion: 1972. Original Cost: $4,600,000.)

The construction of the new Meany Hall completed the Central Plaza ensemble of space and form, but the building would prove to have a troubled future. Designed by the same firm as the Odegaard Library, it shares similar design qualities, such as concrete structure and brick veneer. However, the large interior spaces that it encloses inevitably make for a blocky and rather overbearing presence. Fortunately, the topography allowed the building to be set a level below the plaza, thus softening its visual impact. Inside Meany Hall is the twelve-hundred-seat Meany Theater, which is popular for its spatial and acoustical quality. The building also houses a smaller studio theater, dance studio, offices, lounges, rehearsal rooms, and instrument and costume storage; it has proved to be an important performing arts resource for the University and the community.

Meany Hall's 1994 facelift assisted in warming its welcome as a member of the Central Plaza family. The building had experienced some severe technical problems, particularly water seepage that had weakened the brick veneer facing and its connections with the building's reinforced concrete shell. In preparing to replace the veneer, the architects developed designs for brick patterning and other design modifications that have done much to enhance the visual role Meany Hall plays on the plaza and make it a better neighbor. (Architect: Kirk, Wallace, McKinley & Associates; 1994 rehab, Hewitt Isley. Date of Completion: 1974. Original Cost: $7,122,884; exterior renovation, $9,150,000.)

The central sector includes one other building, not truly a part of the Central Plaza family but close by and a venerable member of the campus family, the Henry Art Gallery. Located just north of the statue of Washington, The Henry (as it is familiarly known) was built with donated funds—among the first such gifts received by the University. The benefactor was Horace C. Henry, whose money came from real estate and railroad interests, but whose business acumen did not preclude an interest in art: there were some 158 pictures in his collection. At a time when there was no art museum in Seattle, Henry opened his home for the public to view his collection. Henry's social circle included President Suzzallo and Carl Gould. The president

LEFT: Meany Hall, 1995
Photo: Stewart Hopkins
ABOVE LEFT: Demolition of Meany Hall following the earthquake damage sustained in 1965
Photo: The Seattle Times, photo archive
ABOVE RIGHT: The original Meany Hall was one of the permanent structures that remained following the AYPE.
Photo: University of Washington Libraries, Special Collections and Preservation Division
OVERLEAF: Central Plaza, with Odegaard Undergraduate Library on the left and Kane Hall on the right
Photo: Chris Eden/Eden Arts

TOP: The Henry Art Gallery expansion as rendered in 1995
Photo: The Henry Art Gallery
ABOVE: The Henry Art Gallery as built in 1927
Photo: University of Washington Libraries, Special Collections and Preservation Division

(and no doubt the architect) appreciated the benefits that might accrue to the University should Henry be induced to donate his art as the foundation of a University museum collection, together with funds for its housing. This Suzzallo was successful in achieving in 1926: $100,000 for the building, together with the paintings, which were appraised then at some $400,000 to $500,000. From those beginnings, the collection and reputation have grown through the years, and The Henry is now a museum with a distinguished national reputation.

The site chosen for the building had in the Regents Plan been identified as part of a substantial public assembly center, including in its core old Meany Hall—an ensemble clearly suggesting a focus on the arts. Adjacent to Meany and with easy public access, the site chosen for The Henry could readily be incorporated into any future plans for expansion and development of the center. The building itself was designed as a simple two-story structure, rectangular and windowless. Its basic simplicity was relieved by the patterning of materials and selected cast-stone details, such as the allegorical figures composed about the main entrance by Dudley Pratt, the exterior niches, and the figures incorporated at the building's four upper corners. These included cast-stone designs representing Ancient Egypt, Greece, Medieval Europe, and Asia. Although at first glance it appears to be another essay in collegiate Gothic, in fact it comes close to being a harbinger of Gould's Art Deco work of the 1930s. Internally, it houses a series of galleries on the main floor, with offices, work areas, and storage on the lower floor. Its fireproof construction throughout was a point of pride.

The Henry is in the planning stages of a thirty-thousand-square-foot expansion. This $15.4 million project not only will provide additional exhibition galleries but also will feature an outdoor plaza and sculpture court, a new entrance lobby and bookstore, administrative offices, auditorium/classrooms, handling and storage facilities, and the renovation of the existing building, which remains as an important visual feature in the project. Additionally, the project's location gives it the opportunity to create an important symbolic visual entry to the main campus from Campus Parkway. (Architect: Bebb and Gould; Current addition: Gwathmey Siegel and Associates and Loschky, Marquardt & Nesholm. Date of Completion: 1927. Original Cost: $100,939.)

Central East Sector

This largest of the campus sectors extends from the perimeter of Liberal Arts Quad and the Allen Library eastward across Montlake Boulevard to include the distant Center for Urban Horticulture. In the HUB Yard one finds the newest of the University's designed open spaces. At the time of the AYPE this area had three major buildings, the Washington and Oregon buildings and the Forestry Building, all facing Nome Circle. By the late 1980s, the latter two buildings and Nome Circle were long gone and only a remnant of the Washington Building still stood. It had first been used (after the AYPE) as the University library; with the 1926 completion of Suzzallo Library it became the Washington State Museum, increasingly dilapidated as the years went by. When the museum moved to its new campus quarters in 1962, the old building disappeared at last, except for a former stack-area appendage that was seen as still having some useful purpose. The area to its north had become an informally landscaped setting with trees, many of which were planted as an International Grove by thirty-five Seattle foreign consuls to celebrate the 1932 bicentennial of George Washington's birth. All in all, what came to be called HUB Yard was largely the result of happenstance, a leftover with no particular design coherence, to say nothing of a designed identity.

This would change with the Allen Library project, part of whose design program was to bring coherence to the yard. The yard itself would, in turn, be redesigned to become a spatial and landscaped campus feature, joining those that were already playing that traditional campus role. Thus, the new building, with its arcade and southeast wing, joined the HUB, Sieg Hall, and new brick walls and lighted gate piers to enclose and define the yard. It has deservedly become a communal gathering place, for planned events or spontaneous sunning and casual conversation.

Facing HUB Yard from the east, in a location roughly that of the AYPE timber-structured Forestry Building, is the Student Union Building, the HUB, or Husky

Union Building. Built after the war as a replacement for the inadequate prewar center in Clark Hall, the building was planned with the help of both student-chaired and membership committees and paid for with ASUW (student) funds.

The HUB is something of a barometer of changing architectural taste, through eight separate phases of construction designed by six different architectural firms from 1948 to 1982. Its earliest construction somewhat conformed to collegiate-Gothic standards, but later work, released from those constraints, sought more individuality. Note the very 1960s folded roof plates of the central body of the building and the 1977 cafeteria expansion overlooking Stevens Way on the east. The HUB houses a full range of student services as well as facilities for the general campus community: eating places, entertainment, a bookstore branch, a barber shop, meeting rooms, student-government offices, and the like.

On the fireplace wall of the second-floor lounge is a nostalgic mural painted by Ernest Norling in 1948 that features a panoply of people and views from University history: Coach Gil Dobie; Hiram Conibear, who invented the winning UW rowing stroke; Clara McCarty holding her diploma (the first issued by the University); Regent Kellogg with his umbrella; a husky dog; the Chimes Tower; and the laying of the Denny Hall cornerstone. (Architects: Bebb and Jones; Jones and Bindon; Bindon and Wright; Tucker & Shields; Joyce, Copeland, Vaughan & Nordfors; and Clayton R. Joyce Architects. Date of Original Completion: 1949. Original Cost: $1,265,000, with both ASUW and University funds; 1977 addition, $5,958,517.)

The last building enclosing HUB Yard is Sieg Hall to the southwest, without doubt everyone's choice for least-favorite campus building. Its self-conscious "modern" verticality and patterning is ironic in that it is a building named for Lee Paul Sieg (University president from 1934 to 1946), who with the architect John Paul Jones was a consistent supporter of the collegiate-Gothic standard for upper campus. The building is a mockery of his values. It presently houses the Department of Computer Science and Engineering. (Architect: Harmon, Prey & Dietrich. Date of Completion: 1960. Original Cost: $1,140,418.)

To the north is another aspect of the Allen project, the replanned Grieg Garden. This charming, quiet retreat, in one of the most densely developed and used parts of the campus, is a wonderful bonus. The garden is focused on a bronze bust of the Norwegian composer Edvard Grieg, a work by Finn H. Frolich from the AYPE. In 1917, it was given to the University by the Scandinavian Societies of the Northwest and Alaska. Unexplained is why Grieg's nose is shiny, since, unlike the toe of Saint Peter's statue in Rome, it remains well out of reach of caressing hands!

Also found in the area of the garden are some fine mature trees, mostly from the 1932 International Grove: a blue spruce, a sugar maple, and a Spanish chestnut. Several European white birches (appropriately part of Grieg's setting) and a European larch have since been planted here. South of the walls near Thomson Hall is a beautiful copper beech, and westward, toward Allen, is a simply splendid Atlas cedar with a spectacular spread to its long curved and gracefully gesticulating branches, like the arms of a ballet dancer. (Landscape Architects: Hanna/Olin, Ltd., and Robert Shinbo. Date of Completion: 1990. Original Cost: $2,275,000.)

Close to Grieg Garden and just across King Lane is Thomson Hall; beyond and attached to it, to the northeast, is the Communications Building. Neither building has any architectural distinction—they are thin, lingering, and probably relatively economical collegiate-Gothic want-to-bes. Essentially classrooms and offices, Thomson Hall also shelters on its top floor the Henry M. Jackson School of International Studies. The building's namesake, David Thomson, is reputed to have held more positions during his tenure (1902 to 1947) than anyone else in University history—professorships, deanships, a vice presidency, and the position of acting Uni-

versity president. Thomson was the first campus building for which the University hired an architect from outside Seattle. The Communications Building, attached to the north, houses the School of Communications and, on its ground floor, the handsomely remodeled Undergraduate Advising Center and the dean's offices for the College of Arts and Sciences. (Architects for both buildings: Heath, Gove & Bell/ Lea, Pearson & Richards. Date of Completion: Thomson, 1948; Communications, 1951 and 1955. Original Cost: Thomson, $849,720; Communications, $406,409 and $1,526,180.)

Just beyond the Communications Building to the north is Clark Hall, which, like its Lewis Hall sibling farther on, retains much the same appearance externally as when it was completed in 1899. But its interiors have been thoroughly sanitized like those of Lewis by successive remodelings, except for some picturesque newel posts. It was a women's dorm until 1936, then served as the first Student Center until the availability of the new HUB in 1952. Lewis and Clark halls were the two dormitories for which the state legislature appropriated $50,000, with a special appropriation added to cover the cost of furnishings. Renamed Lyon Hall in 1903 (for unknown reasons), Clark was lent to the Navy in 1917 as an officers' hospital; five local fraternity houses were leased as women's dorms to replace it. As the center since 1952 for the University's four ROTC programs, Clark Hall provoked student protest in the 1960s and 1970s, and was fire-bombed in 1969. (Architect: Josenhans & Allan. Date of Completion: 1899. Original Cost: $25,000.)

Between Clark Hall and the neighboring Communications Building is a true historic campus tree, an American elm referred to as the Washington elm because it is a scion of the tree in Cambridge, Massachusetts, under which George Washington took command of the Continental Army in 1775. The replacement for an earlier Washington elm that had been struck by lightning, the University of Washington campus tree in due course fathered a replacement for the Cambridge elm, which had been destroyed by a storm.

ABOVE: Grieg Statue, a bronze casting by Finn H. Frolich
Photo: Stewart Hopkins
OVERLEAF: Husky Union Building, the HUB
Photo: Stewart Hopkins

Across Stevens Way from the elm is the most idiosyncratically planned building on campus: Padelford Hall. Its name honors Frederick M. Padelford, who joined the English faculty in 1901, chaired that department until being named dean of the Graduate School in 1926, and filled that post until his death in 1942. The design lineage of this building is clear: it derives from the 1958–62 Ezra Stiles and Morse colleges at Yale, designed by Eero Saarinen, which had a certain design repute at the time in the architectural press. Padelford Hall demonstrates the same quirkiness of plan that is found in the earlier buildings, although in Padelford's case this can be partly accounted for by the site. The building occupies the former location of the AYPE's open-air amphitheater, into whose bowl the building and its lower levels of parking rather ingeniously fit. But the interior space plan can be disorienting.

Nevertheless, as an Arts and Sciences office building, Padelford Hall manages to serve the needs of a disparate group of faculty in English, comparative literature, Romance languages, mathematics, linguistics, and various specialized undergraduate programs, as well as the Mathematics Research Library. (Architect: Walker/McGough. Date of Completion: 1967. Original Cost: $5,013,093.)

Hall Health Center has been serving student health needs since its initial construction in 1936 (with an addition to the east forty years later). Originally, the health center was located in a two-story building on the site of the present stadium. David C. Hall, a physician whom the present building's name honors, was for many years the University's health officer, as well as a professor of hygiene. From his arrival in 1908 until his retirement forty years later, Hall was a campus advocate for the good

ABOVE: Clark Hall was completed in 1899 at a cost of $25,000.
Photo: Chris Eden / Eden Arts
RIGHT: Padelford Hall was completed in 1967 at a cost of $5,013,093.
Photo: Stewart Hopkins

The AYPE amphitheater in 1909, later selected as
the building site for Padelford Hall
*Photo: University of Washington Libraries, Special
Collections and Preservation Division*

life, setting an activist example by playing handball, hiking, and running (he was a runner in the 1900 Paris Olympic Games). (Architect: A. H. Albertson, Wilson & Richardson. Date of Completion: 1936. Original Cost: $200,000, including funds from WPA of $156,000 and SERF of $36,000; 1978 addition, $3,070,000.)

South of Hall Health Center, on Stevens Way, is the Faculty Center, the finest campus example of that architectural design inspiration known as the International Style. Representative of a style noted for its austere formal geometry and its use of modern materials and technology, the center was inspired by the innovative work of certain early-twentieth-century European architects, especially those who came to teach and practice in this country before and following the Second World War. The earlier design traditions enforced on this campus would have resisted the style's intrusion here, and even when those constraints were removed, the initial results were uncertain: e.g., the business school buildings and the 1960s Suzzallo Library addition. But the Faculty Center avoids missteps and demonstrates how much the idiom offers if managed with a sure hand. While the building does not fit the prevailing taste for contextualism, its merits as architecture, as well as its location, fully justify its presence here. The dining-room windows look east to wonderful views of Lake Washington and the distant Cascades.

The building's site is that of the former AYPE Hoo-Hoo House, a clubhouse and meeting place for lumbermen visiting the Exposition. Afterward, the Hoo-Hoo

House became the University's faculty club until its replacement by the present building, the only reminder of the old house being its picture and some of the dark rough-sawn paneling in the downstairs bar. At the time of its razing in 1959, there were still separate entrances for men and women. Some of the Oriental rugs originally from Hoo-Hoo House days, as well as the fireplace andirons, are now in the Faculty Center. The gold sculpture above the main-lounge fireplace is the work of Everett DuPen of the Art School. (Architects: Paul Hayden Kirk & Associates and Victor Steinbrueck. Date of Completion: 1960. Original Cost: $345,637.)

East of and below both the Hall Health Center and the Faculty Center is Fluke Hall, built for the 1983 legislature-mandated Washington Technology Center. The

Fluke Hall, also known as the Washington
Technology Center, was completed in 1990.
Photo: Stewart Hopkins

purpose of the WTC is to develop commercially promising technologies and to expedite their transfer to Washington companies in emerging technological areas—all with a view to expanding the state's economic base. The building is expressive of a program in transition. The west half of the building, against the slope of the site, is "permanent" in its concrete frame and brick construction, housing the administrative activities of the center. The east half, however, is modular in construction, with a wall-panel enclosure that allows for easy expansion should its research activities (whose exact spatial dimensions are usually of an uncertain quantity) require additional space. The name of the building acknowledges the $5 million donation to the WTC by the Fluke family. (Architect: NBBJ. Date of Completion: 1990. Original Cost: $10,000,000.)

Eastward from HUB Yard, down the steps of Wahkiakum Lane, just north of Hall Health Center, across the overpass at Montlake Boulevard, and through the parking lots and sports fields, one comes to the University's Ecological Research Natural Area (ERNA). This expanse below the east slopes of the campus and stretching eastward toward Laurelhurst was all once part of Lake Washington, either under water or as wetlands. But in 1917, with completion of the Lake Washington Ship Canal, the level of the lake dropped and a new shoreline and acreage were created. Beginning in 1926, the area was used as a landfill. People who experienced those times still have vivid memories of swirling smoke and sea gulls, the roar and rattle of dump trucks, and the sight and smells of flames and city refuse. But that activity came to a halt in 1966, when the refuse was capped with earth fill, the west half largely developed for playfields and parking, and the easterly portions of the fill declared an undeveloped biodiverse wildlife sanctuary. The area is now a landscape dominated by grasses, Himalayan blackberries, Scotch broom, a scattering of spontaneous tree and woody shrub clusters, several ponds, and resident or transitory ducks, geese, herons, ospreys, bald eagles, many smaller birds, rabbits, and some northwestern pond turtles. A new interpretive trail was recently established to guide and inform visitors to the area. This and various research beds are parts of the area's ongoing program of site restoration, with zones of varying degrees of management from aggressive to none at all.

To the northeast of the ERNA is the Center for Urban Horticulture, under whose jurisdiction the ERNA operates. The center, itself a division of the College of Forest Resources, is a research and teaching program specializing in plants specifically geared to urban environments, the first and largest such program in the United States. It justly prides itself on having developed a physical plant whose five successive construction phases were funded entirely by donations. The result is a complex of teaching, research, and administrative facilities, most of which cluster about a pleasantly landscaped inner courtyard. A $1 million donation from the local Douglas family made possible the center's Douglas Research Conservatory, which has state-of-the-art facilities for plant propagation, research, and horticultural education; its greenhouses were Dutch-fabricated and assembled on the site. Besides the center's offices, laboratories, greenhouses, and work/storage sheds, there are substantial meeting areas serving broadly based professional and community groups and interests, including a cooperative arrangement for sharing its facilities with the Washington State University/King County Cooperative Extension. The center's Elisabeth C. Miller Library was paid for and endowed by Pendleton Miller and is named for his late wife, a noted Seattle gardener. Wedding receptions are familiar events at the center and in its courtyard. (Architect: Jones & Jones. Date of Completion: 1982–1989. Original Cost: $13,000,000.)

Central South Sector

Architecture Hall stands southeast of the Northeast Fortieth Street entrance to the campus. (This is the same one used for the AYPE.) The hall is the last major building remaining from the Exposition. Built of the same cream-colored brick as the Exposition's much larger Auditorium Building (later, old Meany Hall), and of similar design, this was the Fine Arts Building. As one of the permanent buildings designated to be handed over to the University after the Exposition, it had been designed and equipped to become the Chemistry Building. Subsequently renamed Bagley Hall, the building later became Physiology Hall from 1937 until 1957, when it was given its present name at the founding of the College of Architecture and Urban Planning.

The architecture program had occupied parts of the building since 1937; it shared the space with several other departments, including physiology. During that period, the building's lower floor was noted for the formaldehyde fumes rising from a room that was used for dissections by physiology students. Observed one student, "The only thing we don't like about this place is what's below us. Formaldehyde and bones, screeching animals and eery corpses." The building subsequently underwent two remodelings. The one in 1987 was the most substantial, doing much to restore

ABOVE: Center for Urban Horticulture
Photo: Stewart Hopkins
RIGHT: When the Lake Washington Ship Canal was completed in 1917, nearly one hundred acres of new land was added to the campus. From left: Salmon Homing Pond, the Child Development and Mental Retardation Center, and the Montlake Bridge.
Photo: Wayne Bartz/Tony Stone Images

the building and properly acknowledge its status on the state's list of historic structures. Architecture Hall now houses the college's Department of Building Construction, various architecture studios, some general-purpose classrooms, faculty offices, and a large auditorium. There is a main-floor gallery that features displays of current student work, as well as a popular student-run coffee shop on the top floor.

The coffee shop has a provocative social history. Established in the early 1960s through student initiative, it was considered by the University an inappropriate competitor for HUB facilities. Although its use was officially discouraged, it persisted sub rosa. However, in the turmoil of the late 1960s and beyond, coffee shops suddenly were perceived by the administration as a pacifying presence in a campus atmosphere all too divided and quarrelsome. Thus, this coffee shop was granted respectability, and when the college's students, faculty, and staff moved into their new Gould Hall in 1971, another coffee shop was waiting to serve them as an accepted part of Gould's facilities. (Architect: Howard & Galloway; 1987 remodeling, Boyle-Wagner Architects. Date of Completion: 1909. Original Cost: $216,794; 1987 remodeling, $2,800,000.)

Facing Architecture Hall is Cunningham Hall, which also has an interesting history. Originally the Women's Building for the AYPE, the "temporary" wood-frame and stucco structure, elaborate but insubstantial, was meant to be removed after the Exposition closed. Perhaps because of administrative inertia, the building lingered on, serving a succession of short-term users: the Bureau of Mines, chemistry annex, Air Force ROTC, atmospheric science annex, and architecture. It is the sole remaining temporary AYPE building. The stucco exterior, which had long since deteriorated, was eventually replaced by wood siding. The building's removal was recommended in 1974, when it was declared dilapidated. But by then, the tearing down of a building with links to campus history and the advancement of women was deemed incorrect. In 1979, the building was fully rehabilitated, renamed in honor of Imogen Cunningham, the internationally noted photographer and UW graduate, and designated the campus Women's Center. (Architect: Saunders & Lawton; 1979 rehab, The Hastings Group. Date of Completion: 1909. Original Cost: unknown; 1979, $356,000.)

Science Quad

Eastward are Johnson Hall and (old) Physics Hall, a pair of buildings that define the axis of Rainier Vista as it runs southeast from Grant Lane. Johnson Hall was named for Orson B. Johnson, professor of physiology, botany, zoology, biology, mineralogy, geology, chemistry, and natural philosophy. His affectionate students gave him the

LEFT: Architecture Hall is the last "permanent" building remaining from the AYPE.
Photo: Stewart Hopkins
ABOVE: The AYPE Women's Building remains to this day on campus as Cunningham Hall.
Photo: Documentary Book Publishers, archive

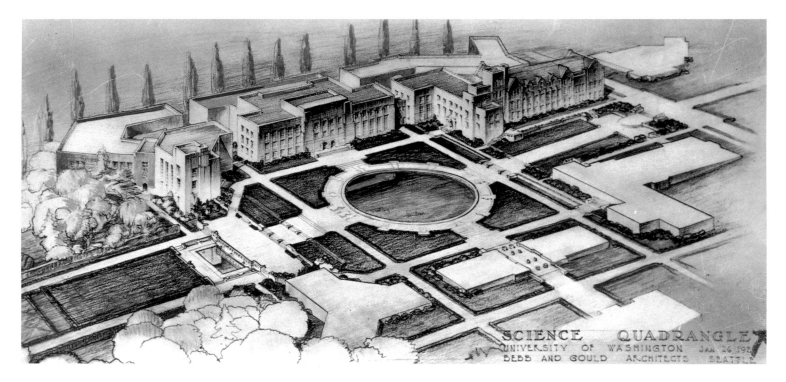

Bebb and Gould's 1920s Science Quadrangle plan
Photo: University of Washington Libraries, Special Collections and Preservation Division

nickname Bug, in recognition of his notable insect collection. He retired in 1910, after twenty-eight years. Johnson Hall serves a variety of the sciences, with labs and classrooms for such disciplines as geophysics, astronomy, botany, and geological sciences.

Since both structures were built as science facilities and are on lower campus, they would seem to be technically immune to the collegiate-Gothic dictates of the upper campus. However, the architects (and no doubt the Board of Regents) were content to let that rule prevail here as well (and the buildings do make a comfortable transition from Central Plaza to whatever would develop southward). Though they match each other in massing and materials, each is individual enough to avoid regimentation. Together they establish a firm sense of continuity for Rainier Vista and also the northerly perimeter of Science Quadrangle.

Hidden away behind Johnson Hall, and also attached to it, are the Atmospheric Sciences-Geophysics Building and Quaternary Research Building, much of the latter underground, with facilities to accommodate those specialized interests. Until 1994, Physics Hall was home base for the Departments of Physics and Astronomy and their library. But both have now moved into the new Physics/Astronomy Building, and planning is under way for the renovation and future uses of Physics Hall, which in 1995 was renamed Mary Gates Hall in memory of a much beloved regent. (Architect: Johnson and Physics halls, John Graham; ASG and QR buildings, Durham, Anderson & Freed. Date of Completion: Johnson Hall, 1930; Physics Hall, 1928; ASG Building, 1970; QR Building, 1973. Original Cost: Johnson Hall, $455,000; Physics Hall, $466,220; ASG Building, $2,110,476; QR Building, $1,389,621.)

Rainier Vista, partly framed by Johnson and Mary Gates halls, is the most sacred space on campus. The vista was first conceived as a centerpiece of the campus plan by the Olmsted Brothers in 1906, when the elusive mountain revealed itself during the firm's visit to Seattle to develop a plan for the AYPE. Rainier Vista is the most dramatic borrowing from nature on any campus in the United States, with Mount Rainier as its climax, and with both architecture and landscape reinforcing its thrust past a minor view of the city toward the mountain beyond. As Edmond Meany put it, "No campus in all the world can equal Rainier Vista. In those rare moments when Mother Nature in kindly mood pulls aside the vaporous curtains we may gaze upon Mt. Rainier, a three-mile . . . flow. . . of rock and ice. A spectacle of unending fascination!"

Between Johnson and Mary Gates halls, the vista crosses to the heart of Science Quadrangle. Its focal point is Frosh Pond and Drumheller Fountain, where the Arc-

ABOVE: Rainier Vista
Photo: Stewart Hopkins
BELOW: Kirsten Wind Tunnel
*Photo: University of Washington Libraries, Special
Collections and Preservation Division*

tic Circle and its round Geyser Basin pool and fountain were located by the Olmsteds for the AYPE. Framed at that time by flowered beds was an elaborate water cascade that stepped down the vista from the elevation of the Court of Honor before the U.S. Government Building to the pool. A broad and nondescript walkway now replaces it. The name Frosh Pond recalls the campus tradition of tossing into its waters freshmen and other unwary candidates for doubtful recognition. The pond has also been the locale for the forestry students' logrolling competition. The fountain was given by regent Joseph Drumheller at the time of the University's centennial celebrations in 1961.

East of Frosh Pond is Guggenheim Hall, home of the Department of Aeronautics and Astronautics, another lower-campus example of collegiate Gothic, and a relatively rich one besides. In 1927 the Daniel Guggenheim Fund donated $292,000 toward construction of a building that would promote aeronautics and "assist in making air transportation safe, popular, and regularly available"; the state was to pay for equipping and staffing the building. Death came to Guggenheim in 1930; he was never to see the building he largely financed. (Architect: John Graham. Date of Completion: 1929. Original Cost: $339,859.)

Behind Guggenheim Hall is the Kirsten Wind Tunnel and Aeronautical Laboratory, called the Wind Tunnel until its name was changed in 1963 to honor

Frederick K. Kirsten, a faculty member from 1915 to 1952 and a holder of over one hundred patents. The building was designed to test aircraft and other structures at speeds of up to 250 miles per hour. (Architect: Bebb and Gould. Date of Completion: 1937. Original Cost: $149,650, with joint funding by UW, Boeing, WPA, and a federal jobs-creation program.)

South of Guggenheim Hall is the Aerospace and Engineering Research Building, its almost windowless brick walls enclosing four floors of test chambers, laboratories, faculty offices, and areas for gas mechanics, wave propagation, and antenna research. (Architect: Young, Richardson and Carleton. Date of Completion: 1969. Original Cost: $1,516,240; 1990 addition, $1,742,000.)

South of the Aerospace Building is the Electrical Engineering Building, designed by one of Seattle's principal architects, the late Paul Thiry, '28, who had an important role in shaping the planning of the campus (as Part One explains). Strictly in the modernist mode—no collegiate Gothic for Thiry!—it has the same modern design lineage as the Faculty Center, though it is here expressed in quite different terms. For the building's exterior walls Thiry specified three Everett DuPen relief panels, which he hoped would somehow express the power of electricity. The sculptor, however, chose more conventional motifs. A fourth floor was added to the building in 1972. Construction is now proceeding to entirely rebuild and extend its west wing. This will create what will be called the Electrical Engineering/Computer Sciences Building, which will reach toward Frosh Pond and establish a configuration similar to—and in concert with—the new Chemistry addition to the west. When completed, the two will create a southerly architectural perimeter for Science Quad and another gateway for the south continuation of Rainier Vista, in ways already demonstrated when one looks northward toward Johnson and Mary Gates halls and beyond. (Architects: Paul Thiry; 1995 expansion, Kallmann McKinnell & Wood and Mahlum & Nordfors. Date of Completion: 1948. Original Cost: $953,464; total expansion project cost, $95,791,000.)

Just south of Electrical Engineering is the tree-framed Sylvan Theater. During the AYPE this was the site of the Music Pavilion, a Greek temple that is long gone. Today, four Ionic columns, hand-carved of cedar, dominate the space, remnants of the old Territorial University Building downtown that were brought to this campus in 1911, when the old building was torn down. The columns were first placed below

Denny Hall on the King Lane axis, but by 1924 they had been moved to the Sylvan Theater, where early commencements were held. Although the columns are original, the capitals are not; they are fiberglass replacements for the originals, which were weathered beyond repair. Meany, who was instrumental in the columns' preservation (he tried to preserve the whole building), and his colleague Herbert T. Condon named them Loyalty, Industry, Faith, and Efficiency, giving us the acronym LIFE.

Bagley Hall, west of Frosh Pond, was named for Daniel Bagley, a Methodist minister whose unpopular anti-slavery position forced him to leave his home in Peoria, Illinois, and move himself and his family to the friendlier social climate of Seattle. Bagley became known as "the man who stole the University for the City of Seattle." As explained in Part One, he worked closely with Arthur Denny, his fellow legislator, to induce the territorial legislature to consider Seattle as a possible site for the University.

Bagley's name had been given first to the AYPE's Fine Arts Building after the University took over the building to house its chemistry program. It was later given to the new Chemistry Building, which was the University's most expensive construction project before the Second World War. Carl Gould worked on the preliminary planning, though he was not the architect of record. The building's design was a modernist concession to the collegiate-Gothic tradition. The lobby's two large linoleum mosaic murals by Robert B. Inverarity offer a more Art Deco treatment. A 1936 WPA Federal Art Project, the murals depict the contributions of Egyptian alchemy and modern science to chemistry. Bagley Hall's principal occupant continues to be the Department of Chemistry.

The Chemistry Building, Bagley's huge new wing to the south, is a major element in the University's program of renewing its science teaching and research facilities. The wing is sited partly to maintain a secondary radial vista along Garfield Lane from the fountain south toward Stevens Way and beyond (and vice versa). But its forward tower and eastward wing also form what will be (with completion of the new Electrical Engineering/Computer Sciences Building) the other half of the defining southwest perimeter to Science Quad, as well as the architectural and landscaping gateway aligned with Rainier Vista that aims toward distant Mount Rainier. Some substantial landscaping south of the building includes reconfigured planting beds for the Medicinal Herb Garden, made necessary by the new construction. (Architects: Naramore, Granger & Thomas with Carl Gould; 1994 addition, Moore, Ruble, Yudell with Loschky, Marquardt & Nesholm. Date of Completion: 1937, 1995. Original Cost: $1,217,000; 1995 addition, construction only, $24,600,000.)

Behind Bagley is Benson Hall, originally known as the Chemical Engineering Building. In 1967 it was renamed to honor Professor Henry K. Benson, a wood-pulp scientist who made important contributions to utilizing this state's major natural resource. His tenure from 1904 to 1954 included chairmanship of his department. The building houses the Department of Chemical Engineering and was designed especially to accommodate the complex scientific instruments needed for the various research activities of its occupants. An important part of its funding came from a National Science Foundation grant. (Architect: Bindon and Wright. Date of Completion: 1966. Original Cost: $2,807,421.)

From Frosh Pond, Island Lane leads south through a wooded grove, a remnant from the early forested days of the campus site, arriving at Stevens Way and the east beds of the Medicinal Herb Garden. It was created in 1911 by the Department of Pharmacy, which in those days was much committed to herbs as a key source of pharmaceuticals; thus they were a subject of the curriculum. Gradually displaced by other priorities in the School of Pharmacy, the garden became something of an orphan until recent years, when it came under the protection of the volunteer group

ABOVE: The Herb Garden and the new Chemistry Building
Photo: Mary Levin, University of Washington, News and Information
OVERLEAF, FROM LEFT: The new Chemistry Building and Bagley Hall
Photo: Stewart Hopkins

Bloedel Hall
Photo: Stewart Hopkins

Friends of the Medicinal Herb Garden, which has taken the initiative to preserve and nurture it. The garden extends westward along Stevens Way, its main entrance marked by two columns topped with monkeys, the traditional symbol of medicinal herb gardens in medieval Italy.

Opposite Island Lane is Anderson Hall, one of the more elaborate examples of collegiate Gothic on lower campus. Perhaps Agnes H. Anderson, who funded the building as a memorial to her late husband, pioneer lumberman Alfred Anderson, was eager that it be architecturally celebratory for that purpose. The home base of the College of Forest Resources, it is another Bebb and Gould design contribution to the campus. In more recent years it has had two buildings added as neighbors: Winkenwerder Hall, named for Hugo Winkenwerder, the forestry dean from 1912 to 1945, and Bloedel Hall, honoring Julius H. Bloedel, a pioneer lumberman and early donor of scholarships and research funds to the college. Both buildings serve the research and teaching needs of the forestry program; Bloedel Hall also houses the Forest Resources Library. Their designs demonstrate the versatility of timber as a structural and finish material. (Architect: Anderson Hall, Bebb and Gould; Winkenwerder Hall, Grant, Copeland, Chervenak & Associates; Bloedel Hall, GCC&A. Date of Completion: Anderson, 1925; Winkenwerder, 1963; Bloedel, 1971. Original Cost: Anderson, $259,603; Winkenwerder, $600,000; Bloedel, $3,870,048.)

The main on-campus arterial is Stevens Way, a beautifully landscaped boulevard. Along its south-central length are opposing lines of deodar cedars, whose dark evergreen heights and gracefully sweeping branches frame the street handsomely. The candles of the cedar cones are a decorative feature; when they produce pollen in the autumn they leave a yellow-green dust drifting across the ground.

Near the northward head of Stevens Way is the Department of Zoology's Kincaid Hall. Professor Trevor Kincaid was one of the University's "grand old men," joining the UW in 1895 as a staff assistant and retiring as a venerable member of the

faculty in 1942. He was central to the University's initiative in developing its Puget Sound Marine Station at Friday Harbor, on San Juan Island, and introduced Japanese oysters into Willapa Bay, for which we can all feel enormous gratitude! Both Kincaid Hall and nearby Guthrie Hall use a shade of red brick untypical of University tradition. (Architects: John Morse/Clayton and Jean Young. Date of Completion: 1971. Original Cost: $4,681,963.)

The Physics/Astronomy Building is the newest addition to Stevens Way. The landscaped plaza between the two structures serves as a roof over a lower level of laboratories and opens splendidly to views of the Southwest Campus, Lake Union, and the city. This is another example of overall campus design as well as architecture, for the plaza was developed to act as an eventual connector between the Central Campus and the area that lies to its southwest. When the Southwest Campus Plan is realized, the Physics/Astronomy plaza will become an entrance to the campus with a pedestrian bridge overpass spanning Pacific Avenue that aligns with the southwest sector's new orientations of streets, vistas, and buildings. Thus the plaza becomes a spatial link between Central Campus and Southwest Campus and Portage Bay.

The Physics/Astronomy Building demonstrates the effort to draw from the design traditions of the campus in contextual ways but with no obvious collegiate-Gothic references. The architects rely instead on building form and materials, especially the choice of brick, whose color range and patterning are familiar on upper campus. Upon closer inspection, one notices physics formulas carved as decoration in the exterior stone trim; a hydrogen-atom mosaic is in one of the lobbies. Much use is made, too, of a material called fritted glass, onto which patterns ("quasi-crystals," in this case) have been silk-screened with ceramic-based paints. The new building provides its faculty what had for so long been denied them in old Physics Hall: isolated and vibration-free labs, substantial floor-load capacity, adequate power and water, modern lecture halls, and offices that allow clustering together of disciplines.

The Astronomy Building features along its facade a dramatic columned arcade and, on its south-facing exterior end wall, a sundial designed by astronomy professor Woodruff Sullivan. From this decorative detail, both standard and daylight saving time can be read (if one has the patience to figure out the posted instructions). The building's atrium, crowned by a soaring glass cupola that is interestingly expressed on the exterior skyline, features a swinging Foucault pendulum. Below is a round brick-enclosed chamber whose design produces tricks of sound: from the middle you can hear your own echo. (Architects: Cesar Pelli and NBBJ. Date of Completion: 1994. Original Cost: $50,000,000.)

North of the complex is Guthrie Hall, home to the Department of Psychology. It was named in memory of Edwin R. Guthrie, who from 1914 until his retirement in 1956 was on the psychology faculty, as well as being dean of the Graduate School from 1943 to 1951. The building's interior core, surrounded by perimeter offices, is a complex of labs for human and animal research—a building within a building. Guthrie's deeply recessed windows are an effort typical of its time, when architects were moving away from the skin-taut facades of the 1950s to seek more robust designs. (Architect: Bindon, Wright & Partners. Date of Completion: 1973. Original Cost: $3,029,000.)

Guthrie Annex 3 is a crisply designed structure originally built for the home economics department in 1942 as its Home Management House. The architect, a recently deceased member of the architecture faculty, was one of the early designers influenced by the International Style in his residential practice. (Architect: John R. Sproule. Date of Completion: 1942. Original Cost: $38,000 from WPA and UW sources.)

ABOVE: Post-World War II temporary buildings, now Guthrie Annex buildings
Photo: Stewart Hopkins
OVERLEAF: Physics/Astronomy Building
Photo: NBBJ/Timothy Hursley

Physics/Astronomy Building
Photo: Chris Eden/Eden Arts

Central West Sector

West of Fifteenth Avenue Northeast and south of Northeast Forty-first Street is acreage outside of the original campus properties. Previously platted and developed as private property, this land was acquired by the University to accommodate the need to expand its facilities. Acquisition was made possible by Metropolitan Tract (the old downtown campus) income, the city buying the old houses with Federal Urban Renewal funds, and the University buying commercial and waterfront ownerships. For planners it posed the continuing problem of how to bring to this area a level of environmental design that will provide some unity with the Central Campus, a project attacked directly in more recent years.

Schmitz Hall stands rather grandly on its podium overlooking Campus Parkway, across Fifteenth Avenue from the Henry Art Gallery. It was named for Henry Schmitz, University president from 1952 to 1958. Of poured concrete, with an ascending cantilevered design, Schmitz Hall was built to consolidate the various facets of student services administration, such as the University Registrar, Housing and Food Services, the Office of Minority Affairs, the Office of Student Affairs, the Student Counseling Center, and Student Financial Aid. At the west end of the bridge that crosses Fifteenth Avenue Northeast from Central Campus to Schmitz Hall stands Philip Levine's *Dancer with a Flat Hat*, a bronze sculpture pointing helpfully to the stairs leading down to the Schmitz podium. It was a gift to the University from the William G. Reed family, honoring Eleanor Henry Reed. (Architect: Waldron & Pomeroy. Date of Completion: 1970. Original Cost: $2,800,000.)

Across University Way on Northeast Forty-first Street is the picturesque Play-house, built during the Depression as the Seattle Repertory Theater. The building was designed by the noted early Seattle architect Arthur C. Lovelace. Purchased by the University in 1951, it was expanded and remodeled in 1968. On either side of the entry door are mosaic murals by Seattle artist Mark Tobey. Before its remodeling, the tiny entry court, with its fine American elm, was more spacious. The tree survives. (Architect: Arthur C. Lovelace; 1968 project, Nelsen, Sabin & Varey. Dates of Completion: 1931, 1968. Original Cost: 1931, unknown; 1967 renovation, $182,000.)

At the far west end of Campus Parkway is the rather forbidding Condon Hall, where the School of Law, its library, faculty, and students reluctantly took up residence in 1973. Some refer to it as "Condon Penitentiary." Its name honors John T. Condon, a faculty member from 1899 to 1926 and the first dean of the Law School, which was founded in 1899. Comfortable as the school had been for years in its old collegiate-Gothic Condon Hall (now Gowen Hall) on Liberal Arts Quad, it has never really adjusted to the raw concrete surroundings into which it was suddenly thrust. This was the first instance of a major on-campus architectural project being assigned by the University to a firm outside this state. (Howard & Galloway of California had been architects for campus work but that was for the AYPE, and they were appointed by its directors.) Plans are under way to build a new law school

Schmitz Hall and *Dancer with a Flat Hat*
Photo: Stewart Hopkins

back on campus. Design studies are being conducted by Kohn Pedersen Fox and its Seattle affiliate Mahlum & Nordfors McKinley Gordon. (Architects: Mitchell/Giurgola Associates with Joyce, Copeland, Vaughan, Nordfors. Date of Completion: 1973. Original Cost: $5,261,700.)

Across the parkway (the westerly sections of which have trees that were planted as part of a 1961 international forestry congress) are the twelve-story horizontal slabs of Terry-Lander halls. Designed as men's dormitories by the same architects, both buildings are in the 1950s design mode. Built first was Terry Hall, the westernmost of the two, named to honor Charles C. Terry, one of the donors of the Territorial University's downtown campus. Four years later it was joined by Lander Hall, named for Judge Edward Lander, who with Arthur Denny and Terry had given the University its ten-acre downtown campus. Designed originally to house men only, the dormitories are now coeducational, with five hundred students in Terry Hall and six hundred in Lander Hall. (Architect: Young, Richardson, Carleton & Detlie. Date of Completion: Terry Hall, 1953; Lander Hall, 1957. Original Cost: $2,800,000.)

Gould Hall (named, of course, to honor Carl F. Gould), a concrete mass that stands at the corner of University Way Northeast and Northeast Fortieth Street, is friendlier inside than out. Designed to meet the needs of the College of Architecture and Urban Planning, it houses three of the college's departments: architecture, landscape architecture, and urban design and planning—as well as the college library. (The fourth department, building construction, is housed in Architecture Hall, across the street on Central Campus.) The spacious interior atrium, with its coffee shop and overlooking balconies, is a unifying feature that gives the departments a perceptual awareness of each other's activities and helps to break down the barriers that departmentalization tends to create. (Architects: Dan Streissguth and Gene Zema. Date of Completion: 1971. Original Cost: $3,376,100.)

The Burke-Gilman Trail was for many years a railroad right-of-way used, in part, to deliver coal to the University Power Plant. The old rails have been removed and

ABOVE: Condon Hall
Photo: Stewart Hopkins
RIGHT: Condon Hall Law Library
Photo: Stewart Hopkins
OPPOSITE: Gould Hall interior
Photo: Stewart Hopkins

The original Physics Building, above Drumheller
Fountain, was renamed Mary Gates Hall in 1995.
Photo: Charles Krebs/Tony Stone Images

the trail is now paved. Some stretches have been landscaped, providing connections for pedestrians, joggers, and bikers between the city's north end, the University, and regions above Lake Washington and beyond. The trail separates the upper two-thirds of the central west sector from its lower third, which is dominated by student housing. Mercer Hall is a dormitory in two related structures designed for 250 students and named for the University's first professor and temporary president (1861–1863), Asa S. Mercer. (Architect: Royal A. McClure & Co. Date of Completion: 1970. Original Cost: $3,000,000.)

To its east is Stevens Court, for five hundred students, a cluster of lower-density scattered apartment units. Its naming honors Washington's first territorial governor, Isaac I. Stevens, who encouraged the University's founders in their pioneering efforts. (Architects: Phase 1, Michael/Lakeman; Phase 2, Mithun Partners. Date of Completion: Phase 1, 1969; Phase 2, 1993. Original Cost: Phase 1, $5,633,750; Phase 2, $9,700,000.)

During the late 1980s and early 1990s Central Campus received the lion's share of new building construction. These handsome additions, including Allen Library, the Physics/Astronomy Building, and what will be the complete reconstruction of the Electrical Engineering Building, have added more than 850,000 gross square feet to the University's inventory. Because of their architects' contextual approach to design, these buildings have added to the visual richness of the campus.

As has been described, Central Campus includes some of the University's most venerable buildings and spaces. On one hand there is that romantic union of form and space found in the architecture and landscape of Liberal Arts Quad. And just beyond, in sharp contrast, is the environmentally disparate partnership of Central Plaza. It is in turn joined by the drama of Rainier Vista and Science Quad. And most recently there is the achievement of the Physics/Astronomy Building and the promise it holds for future linkage with Southwest Campus developments. All are treasures in an inventory of University campus riches.

CHAPTER EIGHT

South Campus

MORE THAN IN ANY OTHER REGION OF THE UNIVERSITY, THE CHARACTER OF
South Campus buildings reflects their uses. Engineering, athletics, health sciences, oceanography, and fisheries required buildings whose forms were shaped by their function. The health sciences complex and Husky Stadium are massive structures. Still, this largely waterfront area is rich with natural and landscaped beauty.

Southeast Sector

Southeast of the HUB, along Stevens Way, is a sweep of buildings that (along with the Electrical Engineering Building) comprise an enclave of specialized engineering facilities. First are the Engineering Library and Loew Hall, which with the little brick-paved plaza in between were a single design project. Much favored at the time by its architect were the eyebrowed windows and the brick, which draws from a different color range than is typical elsewhere on campus. Loew Hall, the College of Engineering's administrative offices and teaching facility, honors Edgar A. Loew, who came to the engineering faculty in 1909, became dean of the College of Engineering, and retired in 1948. (Architect: Fred Bassetti & Company. Date of Completion: 1969. Original Cost: $3,198,000.)

Farther south on Stevens Way are the nondescript 1950s Mechanical Engineering Building and mid-1940s More Hall, built to house the Department of Civil Engineering. The former occupies the site of the AYPE's Machinery Hall, a permanent structure that became the University's Engineering Hall before its present replacement. The Engineering Annex to the rear still includes construction remaining from its AYPE days. (Architect: ME Building, Carlson, Eley & Grevstad; More Hall, Bebb and Jones, Leonard Bindon, Assoc. Date of Completion: ME Building, 1959; More Hall, 1946. Original Cost: ME Building, $1,542,922; More Hall, $972,000.)

Between More Hall's west face and Stevens Way is a bronze bust of James J. Hill by the sculptor Finn H. Frolich, another of those elements from the AYPE that have come to grace today's campus. A railroad magnate known as the Empire Builder, Hill was central to the successful 1893 efforts to tie Seattle by railroad to the rest of the nation.

Well back from Stevens Way is Roberts Hall, part of the earlier generation of Bebb and Gould work on campus. Its design manages to give collegiate-Gothic dignity to a building devoted to the pragmatic teaching functions of the College of Mines, courses such as ceramic engineering and the treatment and use of coal. Mining engineer Milnor Roberts, the building's namesake, arrived on campus in 1902 and was for many years the college's dean and a generous donor to the University, retiring in 1947. Now housing the Department of Materials Science and Engineering, the building has had a recent, substantial, and handsome redesign for the department's specialized metallurgy research. (Architect: Bebb and Gould; renovation, Duarte Bryant. Date of Completion: 1921, 1988. Original Cost: $127,781, $3,800,000.)

Husky Stadium
Photo: Wayne Bartz / Tony Stone Images

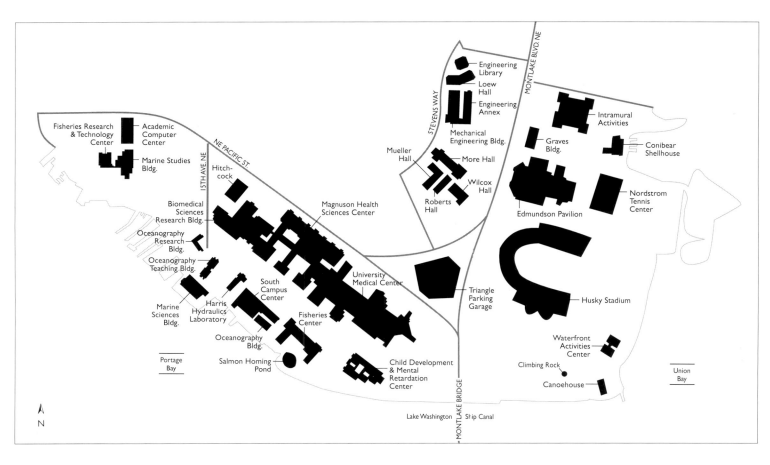

Fisheries Research & Technology Center
Academic Computer Center
Marine Studies Bldg.
Hitch-cock
Biomedical Sciences Research Bldg.
Oceanography Research Bldg.
Oceanography Teaching Bldg.
Marine Sciences Bldg.
Harris Hydraulics Laboratory
Oceanography Bldg.
Salmon Homing Pond
South Campus Center
Fisheries Center
Child Development & Mental Retardation Center
Magnuson Health Sciences Center
University Medical Center
Triangle Parking Garage
NE PACIFIC ST
15TH AVE NE
STEVENS WAY
MONTLAKE BLVD. NE
Engineering Library
Loew Hall
Engineering Annex
Mechanical Engineering Bldg.
Mueller Hall
More Hall
Wilcox Hall
Roberts Hall
Intramural Activities
Graves Bldg.
Conibear Shellhouse
Edmundson Pavilion
Nordstrom Tennis Center
Husky Stadium
Waterfront Activities Center
Climbing Rock
Canoehouse
Portage Bay
Union Bay
MONTLAKE BRIDGE
Lake Washington   Ship Canal
N

When new facilities became necessary to house an expansion, it was decided that, rather than build in front of Roberts Hall and destroy its visual prominence, the department would build down. The resulting Mueller Hall leaves unbroken the vista from Stevens Way to Roberts Hall, while at the same time providing a designed open space around the sunken plaza into which open its subsurface rooms. Its name honors Professor of Mining and Metallurgical and Ceramic Engineering James I. Mueller, who was on the faculty from 1949 to 1973, three of those years as departmental chairman. (Architects: Ralph Anderson; Koch Duarte. Date of Completion: 1986. Original Cost: $2,900,000.)

The Triangle Parking Garage lies—invisibly—just beyond the southeastern end of Rainier Vista. A great hubbub arose when the sign went up announcing that a "garage" would be built on the site. The furor subsided only when the sign was amended to read "underground garage." The episode provided reassurance that both University and community care about the campus and its protection as a splendid design achievement. (Lid Architect: The Bumgardner Architects; Landscape Architect: SWA. Date of Completion: 1985. Garage and Lid Original Cost: $4,100,000.)

Across Montlake Boulevard is the overwhelming presence of Husky Stadium. Dedicated in 1920, the original stadium horseshoe and its uncovered stands were constructed of concrete laid directly on ground that had been shaped by sluicing. The work was financed by a combination of ASUW funds and the sale of plaques and advance seating. Further work in the 1930s added bleachers and provided for facilities such as a head house, ticket office, concessions, broadcast and public-address systems, and spotlights. ASUW funds were used in 1950 to erect the south stands, and in 1988, with much additional donated funding, to erect the north stands, bringing the stadium capacity to 71,600. The north stands' most memorable moment was the collapse of the project's structural steel during construction, an event that, in the opinion of one wag, created the most handsome piece of modern sculpture on campus. But, somehow, the stands were in place for the opening of the 1988 football season.

Of special interest is the redesigning and landscaping of the once-disheveled area between the stadium and Montlake Boulevard. With a design that coordinates with the Triangle Garage landscaping across the boulevard, the space now presents an appropriate image of the University to people either passing by or assembling for sporting events, commencement exercises, or other special occasions. (Architect: Bebb and Gould; 1950 addition, George Wellington Stoddard and Associates; 1988 addition, Skilling Ward Magnusson Barkshire, Inc., engineers, with NBBJ. Dates of Completion: 1920, 1950, 1988. Original Cost: 1920, $577,000; 1950, $1,727,922; 1988, $17,723,050, including site improvements; 1989 west stand replacement cost, $3,685,000.)

Just to the north of the stadium is Edmundson Pavilion, another ASUW-funded project. Known until the mid-1940s as the Men's Athletic Pavilion, it was then renamed to honor Clarence S. "Hec" Edmundson, from 1920 to 1954 a key figure in the University's program for men's physical education. A swimming pool was attached to the east in 1939. Each June, the pavilion is the setting for the University's commencement exercises (now held both morning and afternoon to accommodate the large number of graduates and their guests). The combination of academically gowned faculty and students, thousands of spectators, colorful decorations, and a festive spirit brings to the pavilion an unexpected élan. (Architect: Bebb and Gould. Date of Completion: 1928. Original Cost: $663,000. Swimming Pool Architect: Bebb and Jones. Date of Completion: 1939. Original Cost: $209,420.)

Behind and to the east of Edmundson Pavilion is the Nordstrom Tennis Center, which fills the University's long-standing need for year-round practice and match

TOP LEFT: South Campus map
BOTTOM LEFT: Roberts Hall, 1921, by Bebb and Gould, and the below-ground Mueller Hall, 1986, by Ralph Anderson and Koch Duarte
Photo: Stewart Hopkins
TOP RIGHT: Edmundson Pavilion, 1928, by Bebb and Gould
Photo: The Seattle Times, photo archive
BOTTOM RIGHT: Since its completion as an athletic facility, "Hec Ed" has housed a wide variety of functions, from commencements to conventions. Shown is a 1930s automobile show.
Photo: The Seattle Times, photo archive

The original Shell House
Photo: University of Washington Libraries, Special Collections and Preservation Division

facilities. With six courts, locker and shower facilities for men's and women's teams, meeting room, spectator facilities, and lobby, the center is a gift of the Nordstrom family. (Architect: The McKinley Architects. Date of Completion: 1987. Original Cost: $2,900,000.)

Due north of the pavilion is the Graves Building, which contains athletic offices (named for Dorsett "Tubby" Graves, affiliated with the University from 1922 to 1947), and beyond it is the Intramural Activities Building, a coeducational facility with four gymnasiums, a swimming pool, and other specialized features and offices. Both buildings were designed by the same architect. (Architect: Robert Billsbrough Price Associates. Date of Completion: Graves, 1963; IAB, 1968. Original Cost: Graves, $521,426; IAB, $4,553,000.)

Behind the Intramural Building on the lake shore is the 1949 Conibear Shellhouse, which memorializes rowing coach Hiram Conibear. Conibear originally came to the University as a football trainer and track coach, but by 1907 he found himself coach of rowing, a sport in which he had no previous experience. Nevertheless, his probing analysis of the physiology of rowing led to the creation of the Huskies' winning "Conibear stroke." He died in an accident in 1917. The shellhouse is of no particular interest, except as home base for the renowned UW Crew and its rowing shells. Of greater appeal is the adjoining Shellhouse Annex, which shelters the crew coaches' launches and the rest of the floating-service equipment flotilla. The designer's handling of its low-curved roof and utilitarian structure gives the building an appealing sophistication, quite unexpected in these quarters. The annex has a design precedent for its roofline and structural brackets: the same design was used

Early-morning practice
Photo: Stewart Hopkins

in the old wood-frame ASUW Canoehouse, which for years also housed George Leis and his wife, who staffed the canoe program. Curiously, the designers of the annex claimed to have had no previous knowledge of the old Canoehouse, of which it seems such a clone. (Architects: Kramer, Chin & Mayo with The Miller Hull Partnership. Date of Completion: 1993. Original Cost: $460,000.)

South on Walla Walla Road is the Waterfront Activities Center, built to serve the University's recreation-oriented water sports of sailing, canoeing, and kayaking. With its docks, floats, and piers and the facilities to support its programs, it becomes a busy place, especially when the sun is out and the waterways are calm, or during football season, when many game enthusiasts come by boat and moor at these docks. Its comfortable, rather domestic-scale architecture and upper-level floor (with lounge, meeting room, and large deck) contribute to its popularity, whether for boating or for departmental retreats, reunions, and other special events. (Architect: Donald J. Foote. Date of Completion: 1976. Original Cost: $1,035,102.)

Just to the south of the Waterfront Activities Center is, surprisingly, another of the state's listed historic buildings and the only campus National Registrant: the Canoehouse, facing the ship canal. Frame-constructed with shingled siding, it was originally built in 1918 as a hangar for the Aviation Training Corps, but it was never used as such and was ultimately given to the University as a shellhouse for the rowing crew. When the crew moved its shells to the new shellhouse in 1949, this one became the Canoehouse, used also by the Husky Sailing Club as its boathouse.

(Architect: L. E. Gregory, engineer for Puget Sound Navy Yard. Date of Completion: 1918. Original Cost: $17,455.)

West and just above the Canoehouse is what might offhand be thought of as another campus art piece: Climbing Rock. Although designed as recreation and training for rock climbers, it also deserves honor for its sculptural beauty. (Architect: Anderson & Bell. Date of Completion: 1974. Original Cost: $62,300.)

South Sector

Although dominated by the architectural behemoth of the University's medical facilities, this sector holds more programmatic versatility than would at first appear. But clearly, health sciences are the major activity here, and visitors to the sector will first encounter the challenging vastness of these health sciences facilities, which act as a kind of giant institutional wall paralleling Northeast Pacific Street.

Here we find two major institutions. The western half of the structure is the Magnuson Health Sciences Center, which is dedicated to research and teaching. It was named to honor Washington's U.S. Senator Warren G. Magnuson, who over the course of his long political career was able to steer a great deal of federal financial support to the University's health sciences program, including the Health Sciences Library and Information Center. The balance of the building, to the east, is the University of Washington Medical Center, designed as a partner to the Magnuson Center. Given the enormous commitment of University and state resources these centers represent, and their reputation among the nation's top hospitals and medical schools, it is important to appreciate how relatively new they are in the health sciences world.

The Board of Regents took initial steps toward organizing a school of medicine as early as 1884, but when its initiative received no support from the state legislature, the board's action was repealed. There was no improvement in 1918, when President Suzzallo again formally raised the matter. This proposal was met with a lack of enthusiasm from both the University faculty and the local medical profession, and he had to settle for an agreement whereby Washington medical students could be admitted to the University of Oregon Medical School.

Efforts continued, but they did not reach fruition until after the Second World War, when the University, the medical profession, and the legislature recognized the pressing need for medical education. In 1946, the School of Medicine opened in makeshift quarters, and three years later it moved into its own building on the property above Portage Bay that had been the University's nine-hole golf course. From that 1949 core (essentially that of today's Magnuson Health Sciences Center), the buildings have sprawled in all four directions, creating a scene of almost continuous construction ever since.

The hospital, the first unit of the University of Washington Medical Center, was begun in 1952; its second construction phase provided an eight-story hospital that was completed in 1958. Successive construction projects over the years have added to the bulk of the health sciences buildings as well as to their circulation confusions. The most recent projects, as of this writing, are the southwest H Wing and K Wing additions; the latter constitutes the Biomedical Sciences Research Building, with significant support of $12 million from Microsoft CEO William Gates III. (Original Architects: NBBJ. Date of Completion, A through H Wings: 1949. There have followed successive, almost uninterrupted, additions involving large sums of money and a series of architectural firms, including McClelland & Jones, Bebb and Jones, Waldron Pomeroy Smith Foote and Akira, Caudill Rowlett Scott, Arai/Jackson, TRA, NBBJ, Decker/Fukui Associates, and Mahlum and Nordfors. Date of Completion: 1995. Total Cost: $164,100,000.)

Climbing Rock, designed by Anderson & Bell, was completed in 1974.
Photo: Stewart Hopkins

UNIVERSITY OF WASHINGTON

The architectural design of these successive projects is consistently modern, though expressive of changing tastes over the years. Concrete technology with brick facing was the initial style of choice; later work usually showed greater reliance on concrete alone, augmented by tile facing to give it more color and finish. There is no hint of collegiate Gothic to be found. Sculptured inserts by Dudley Pratt were part of the original 1949 project. A large exterior wall-mounted piece is found along the walk leading to the medical center's original main entrance at the northwest corner of A Wing (composed of a group of people, it has "D. E. Pratt, 1947" inscribed just under a seated male figure). Through the nearby entrance are three smaller pieces of Pratt's work on the wall of the former main lobby.

But, in more recent work, such design flourishes incorporated into the exteriors of the buildings have disappeared; greater reliance has been placed on public art as objects outside or inside the buildings. The Medical Center's main floor houses an extensive collection of paintings, sculpture, and Dale Chihuly glass, all paid for with money earned from the nearby coffee stand. The Patrick Zentz *Stetho,* a sculpture of tubes, cylinder, and tuning forks, produces sounds triggered by human movements in the atrium in which it hangs. From this level, one can also see in the grounds south of the building the Mary Miss untitled earth sculpture, a composition of fences, pergola, bricked walks, and water set in lawns surrounded by a ring of atlas cedars and hemlock. Due south of the Magnuson Center on the grade-level roof of the parking garage north of South Campus Center is another untitled art piece, this one a steel plate sculpture by Robert Maki, composed of three sides and an open end, and open to the sky.

To the west, but separate from the Magnuson Center, is Hitchcock Hall, a brick block with an austerely refined elegance. A research building for biological sciences, it honors Professor C. Leo Hitchcock, a professor of botany who specialized in plants of the Pacific Northwest and taught from 1937 to 1972. (Architect: TRA. Date of Completion: 1981. Original Cost: $14,138,915.)

Along the shoreline of Lake Washington Ship Canal and Portage Bay is a row of other facilities related indirectly or not at all to health sciences. Closest to the Montlake Bridge is the Child Development and Mental Retardation Center, a group of attached buildings of disparate architecture whose one-story easterly classroom wing opens pleasantly south to the canal. (Architect: Arnold D. Gangnes. Date of Completion: 1969. Original Cost: $4,041,607.)

Westward, the Fisheries Center is mostly a 1951 design, but its later red-brick east wing plays interestingly with corbeled brick, producing curved surfaces for roof cornice and "fisheye" windows that angle out toward the view. Of its much-admired design, one critic noted that "it is a far cry from the boxlike anonymity of the now outdated Bauhaus or International Style." The center was built to house the School of Fisheries' offices, classrooms, research laboratories, and fish collection; outside are the Hatchery and Salmon Homing Pond, especially interesting when the school's own run of returning salmon make their seasonal appearance. (Architects: Young and Richardson; Ralph Anderson. Dates of Completion: 1951, 1968. Original Cost: $1,054,000.)

West of Fisheries is the Oceanography Building, pleasantly, even romantically, collegiate Gothic, though stylistically out of place in a sector dominated by various modernist interpretations of contemporary architecture. Funded by a gift from the Rockefeller Foundation, the building contains the School of Oceanography's chemical oceanographic research program. (Architect: John Graham. Date of Completion: 1932. Original Cost: $199,000.)

Oceanography is wrapped closely to the west and north by a dominating neighbor, the South Campus Center. When viewed from the north, this building appears

BELOW: This School of Nursing lecture hall is an example of the technical design requirements of health sciences buildings.
Photo: Jeff Zaruba
RIGHT: Biomedical Sciences Research Building
Photo: Stewart Hopkins

to be a one-story structure, but it steps down along its south-sloping site to become a three-story building whose generous windows face the view and water-based activities of Portage Bay. A boldly reinforced concrete building, the center was built to provide the same range of services on the South Campus that the HUB does for the Central Campus: food services, meeting rooms, a branch of the bookstore, a barber shop, and some recreational areas. (Architect: Bumgardner Partnership. Date of Completion: 1974. Original Cost: $3,000,000.)

The Harris Hydraulics Laboratory, due west, is the one Bebb and Gould contribution to this part of the campus. Along with a 1960 addition, it houses offices and research labs for civil engineering and bioengineering. Charles W. Harris, for whom the building was named, was a professor of civil engineering from 1906 until his retirement in 1951. (Architects: Bebb and Gould; Liddle & Jones. Dates of Completion: 1920, 1960. Original Cost: $63,000, $304,600.)

The west boundary of this sector is substantially established by two adjoining buildings: the Oceanography Teaching Building and, south of it along the Portage Bay shoreline, the Marine Sciences Building. They were designed by the same architectural firm and share a common structural vocabulary of poured and textured concrete, their terraces supported by boldly battered walls that suggest a kind of

TOP: Overshadowed by the health sciences complex, the marine, fisheries, and oceanographic study facilities line the shore of Portage Bay.
Photo: Stewart Hopkins
ABOVE: Marine Sciences Building
Photo: Stewart Hopkins

revetment appropriate to a shoreline location. Those of the Marine Sciences Building are especially telling, with their facing patterns of river rock. The Marine Sciences Building serves the School of Oceanography with research labs and offices; the Oceanography Teaching Building has the department's classrooms, teaching labs, seminar rooms, and more faculty offices, as well as the Fisheries-Oceanography Library. At the Marine Sciences dock one can occasionally find the UW fleet's flagship, the *Thomas G. Thompson,* a 3,051-ton research vessel that was commissioned in 1991, its comings and goings administered by the School of Oceanography. (Architect: Liddle & Jones. Date of Completion: MSB, 1967; OTB, 1969. Original Cost: MSB, $2,052,600; OTB, $1,600,000.)

Until recently, the University's plans for shoreline development in this area were in limbo, but with the approval of the Southwest Campus Plan, and removal of the old Showboat Theater from below South Campus Center, work has begun to move forward. Within the limits of current budget constraints, preliminary landscaping improvements are afoot. Even modest changes here improve the attractiveness of the shoreline and give better public access; further extending the pathway along Portage Bay and the canal, for example, reinforces the relationship between the campus and the waterfront, a unique environmental asset.

Southwest Sector

It is appropriate to conclude this review of the University campus with the southwest sector, as it is the one with the greatest development promise. As detailed in Part One, the approval by various University and municipal groups of the Southwest Campus Plan has opened the area to redesign and development that promise to rescue it from the often dreary reality of its present condition. Axes and vistas will be opened up to Central Campus and to the community, some streets will be replatted, the shorelines of bay and canal will be enhanced and made more accessible, and architectural forms will be created and coordinated to define new open spaces.

The MV *Thomas G. Thompson*, an example
of marine architecture, is a floating classroom and
laboratory for the study of oceanography.
*Photo: Mary Levin, University of Washington, News
and Information*

Some of this rehabilitation has already begun. With a view to the long-range goal of emphasizing the University's water-oriented programs in this sector, the new Marine Studies Building and its connecting Fisheries Research and Technology Center are already in place—in locations designated by the Southwest Campus Plan. Built at different times, they share, nevertheless, a similar technology of poured and precast concrete—the fisheries building benefiting from its later date and a sprightlier design. The Marine Studies Building, home of the School of Marine Affairs, the Division of Aquaculture and Food Science, and the Institute for Food Science and Technology, features in its lobby *A Sea-Time Story,* a 1985 stained-glass window by Dick Weiss, filled with evocations of underwater themes. (Architects: MSB, Streeter Dermanis with NBBJ; FTRC, The Miller Hull Partnership. Date of Completion: MSB, 1984; FTRC, 1990. Original Cost: MSB, $4,599,354; FTRC, $2,581,772.)

Due north of the Marine Studies Building is the Academic Computer Center, an index of the computer's impact on the University community. Its no-nonsense concrete form, with its ramped bridge to the upper floor and rather stark interiors, seems appropriate for tenants and users, mesmerized as they are by the technology of keyboard and screen before them. In addition to ranks of computer stations and servicing facilities, the building includes an Information Center. (Architect: Ibsen Nelsen & Associates. Date of Completion: 1976. Original Cost: $1,719,095.)

These three buildings, as the Southwest Campus Plan indicates, eventually will be part of a larger ensemble oriented around a new shared campus open space, Fisheries Quadrangle. The quad will open onto a rehabilitated waterfront south of Boat Street, with a new Fish Return Pond whose landscaping will extend eastward to join that of Sakuma Viewpoint. This waterfront feature (designed by McLeod Reckord) was developed in memory of Professor of Landscape Architecture Donald Sakuma, who taught from 1963 until his untimely death in 1975. At present, it is the only place on this immediate shoreline that invites people to enjoy the views and life of Portage Bay; the public will find the University's future waterfront far more hospitable.

With the gradual realization of the Southwest Campus Plan, what is now mostly a disheveled area of parking lots and buildings will disappear. The latest heir to the inspiration of the Olmsted Brothers' plan for the 1909 AYPE, the 1915 Regents Plan, and the successive development that the campus has since enjoyed, the southwest sector can look forward to a future in which, to the benefit of both the campus and the community, it takes its rightful place in the drama of environmental design that is the campus of the University of Washington.

The Past and Future Campus

And so has been traced a century of the University of Washington's unfolding history on its Interlaken site. From an acreage generous in scale and wonderfully endowed by nature with water and mountain vistas, and by city views that followed, it has been nurtured into the splendor of a built environment unmatched in the league of university campuses.

Most of what evolved is the result of the work and foresight of generations of people who cared enormously about the University and the extent to which its campus was an index of the values and future they sought for it. Theirs was the vision and achievement of a worthy setting for the University of a Thousand Years. Ours is the responsibility that in the next one hundred years and those to follow, its campus and towers will still stand, its battlements still shine in dawning light, and glow again in sunset rays. All hail! O Washington!

Suggested Reading

Gates, Charles M. *The First Century at the University of Washington, 1861–1961*. Seattle: University of Washington Press, 1961.

Ochsner, Karl Jeffrey. *Shaping Seattle Architecture: A Historical Guide to the Architects*. Seattle: University of Washington Press in association with the American Institute of Architects Seattle Chapter and the Seattle Architectural Foundation, 1994.

Odegaard, Charles E. *The Newcomen Society of North America Address*. New York: The Newcomen Society of North America, June 12, 1963.

Rash, David A. *Viewpoints: University of Washington Campus*. Unpublished manuscript, University of Washington Library, December 20, 1992.

Sanders, Jane. *Into the Second Century: The University of Washington, 1961–1986*. Seattle: University of Washington Press, 1987.

Southwest Campus Plan. Seattle: The University of Washington, April 5, 1993.

Talley, Bill. "Ground for Growing: The University of Washington Campus, 1894–1994." Seattle: *Daily Journal of Commerce,* March 24, 1994.

Three Quarters of a Century at Washington. Seattle: The University of Washington Alumni Association, 1941.

University Relations. *A Campus Walk*. Seattle: University Relations, September 1994.

Index

Numbers in *italic* refer to photographs.

A

A Campus Walk, 95, 100
A Sea-Time Story, 166
Academic Computer Center, 166
Administration Building (before 1949. *See*
    Denny Hall)
Administration Building, 48, 59, 60, 66, 81,
    103, 110–111, *113*. *See also* Gerberding
    Hall
Aerospace and Engineering Research
    Building, 136
Alaska-Yukon-Pacific Exposition, 26, *26*, 27,
    28, *28*, 32, *32*, 37, 53, 56, 72, 103, 119, 124,
    126, *126*, 130, 135, 136, 151
Albertson, A. H., 100
Albertson, Wilson & Richardson, 126
Allen, Kenneth S., 108
Allen Library, 11, 53, *62*, 66, 68, 95, 108, 110,
    110, 111, 122, 149
Allen, Paul G., 108
Alumni House, 84
Ames, Walker (family), 111
amphitheater, 124, *126*
Anderson, Agnes H., 66, 140
Anderson, Alfred, 140
Anderson & Bell, 157
Anderson Hall, *64–65*, 140
Anderson, Ralph, 153, 159
Arai/Jackson, 157
arboretum, Edmond Meany's hopes for, 21,
    44, 82, 84, 101
Arboretum, Washington Park, 95
Architecture Hall, 68–69, 130, *132*, 146
Arctic Circle, 134–135
Arkans, Norman, 7
Art Building, 101, *101*, 103
art on campus, 56, 59
Arthur, John, 18
Arts Quadrangle, 22. *See also* Liberal Arts
    Quadrangle
ASUW, 69, 122, 153, 155

Atmospheric Sciences-Geophysics Building,
    134
Austin, Isabella, 85
Aviation Training Corps, 155
AYPE. *See* Alaska-Yukon-Pacific Exposition

B

Bagley, Clarence, 81
Bagley, Daniel, 10, *15*, 15–16, 18, 81, 137
Bagley Hall, original, 130
Bagley Hall, present, *50*, 137, *138–139*
Bailey, George, 75, *76*
Balmer Hall, 50, 56, 79
Balmer, Thomas, 79
Baptist Student Center, 84
Barnes, Edward Larrabee, 60, 110
Bebb and Gould, 29, 34, *34*, 38, *38*, 39, *39*, 42,
    42, 43, 44, 48, 68, 93, 95, 97, 100, 101,
    106, *106*, 107, 110, 118, 134, *134*, 136, 140,
    151, 153, 162
Bebb and Jones, 110, 122, 151, 153, 157
Bebb and Jones, Leonard Bindon, Associates,
    151
Benson Hall, 137
Benson, Henry K., 137
Bindon and Wright, 110, 122, 137
Bindon, Wright & Partners, 141
Biomedical Sciences Research Building, 157,
    162, *163*
Blaine, Catherine V., 85
Blethen, Colonel Alden J., 22, 75
Bloedel Hall, 140, *140*
Bloedel, Julius H., 140
Boeing Company, The, 136
Boiserie, The, 78
Boone Plan, 20, *20*, 21
Boone, William E., 20
Boyle-Wagner Architects, 133
Broken Obelisk, 56, 106, *113, 116–117*
brutalism, 91, 95
Bumgardner Architects, The, 153, 162
Burke, Caroline McGilvra, 76
Burke-Gilman Trail, 48, 146, 149

Burke Memorial Washington State Museum, 76, 78, 119
Burke, Thomas, 76
Business Administration, 66
By George, 113

C

Campaign for Washington, 63
Campus Green, 83, *83*, 84, 93
Campus Parkway, 29, 48–49, 66, 95
Canoehouse, *68, 69*, 155
carillon, 75
Carlson, Eley & Grevstad, 151
Carnegie Foundation, 13
Carr, Edmund, 15
Cascade Mountains, 21, 27, *88–89*
Caudill Rowlett Scott, 157
Center for Urban Horticulture, 95, 129, *130*
Central Campus, 47, 52, 71, 75, 95, 96 (map), 96–149
Central Plaza, 30, *39*, 42, 52, 60, 66, 103, *104–105*, 110–111, 115, *116–117*, 149
Central Quadrangle. *See* Central Plaza
Chemical Engineering Building. *See* Benson Hall
Chemistry Building, original, 130, 137
Chemistry Building, present, 53, 63, 66, 68, 95, 136, 137, *138–139*
cherry trees, 67, 73, 95
Chiarelli, James J., 78
Child Development and Mental Retardation Center, 131, *131*, 159, *160–161*
Chimes Tower, 75, *76*
Circum Okto, 108
City-University Agreement, 1983, 71
Clark, Alan, 56, 107
Clark Hall, 21, *22*, 69, 72, 122, 123, *124*
Clayton R. Joyce Architects, 122
Climbing Rock, 59, 156, *156*, 157
collegiate Gothic, 29, 30, 31–32, 34, 38, 42, 43, 50, 67, 72, 79, 97, 101, 102, 103, 107, 108, 122, 134, 135, 140, 141, 151, 159
columns, 69, *69*, 136–137
Commerce Hall. *See* Savery Hall
Commons, 95
Condon Hall, original. *See* Gowen Hall
Condon Hall, present, 95, 145, 146, *146*
Condon, Herbert T., 27, 28, 38, 111, 137
Condon, John T., 145
Conibear, Hiram, 122, 154
Conibear Shellhouse, 154
Conrad, Ernest M., 7, 49
contextualism, 67, 73, 79, 95, 108, 110, 141
Conway, John Ashby, 79
Cotterill, George F., 27
Court of Honor, 103, 135
Croonquist, Alfred H., 103
Cunningham Hall, 133, *133*
Cunningham, Imogene, 133

D

Dancer with a Flat Hat, 56, 144, *145*
Daniel Guggenheim Fund, 135
Daughters of the American Revolution, 106
Decker & Christensen, 79
Decker, Christensen and Kitchin, 79
Decker/Fukui Associates, 157
Denny, Arthur A., 10, 15, *15*, 18, 81, 137
Denny, Brewster C., 7, 10, *10*, 11, 81
Denny Field, *23*, 84, 85, 93
Denny Hall, *14*, 15, 21, *21*, *38*, 68, 72, 75, 78, 80, 81, 83, *83*, 93
Denny, Mary, 10
Denny Yard, *81*, 82, 93
Denny's Knoll, 15, 17
dormitories, 21, 43, 44, 85, 123, 146
Douglas family, 129
Douglas Research Conservatory, 129
drill hall, 21
Drumheller Fountain, 32, *33*, 70, 134–135
Drumheller, Joseph, 135
Duarte Bryant Architecture, 151
Duarte Koch, 153
DuPen, Everett, 56, 113, 127, 136
Durham, Anderson & Freed, 134
Duthweiler, Edward, 7

E

Ecological Research Natural Area, 72, 129
Edmond S. Meany sequoia, 101
Edmundson, Clarence S. "Hec", 153
Edmundson Pavilion, 153, *153*
Education Hall. *See* Miller Hall
Electrical Engineering Building, 136, 149
Electrical Engineering/Computer Sciences Building, 63, 66, 136, *136*, 137, 149
Elisabeth C. Miller Library, 129
Elliot, John, 100
Engineering Annex, 151
Engineering Hall, 151
Engineering Library, 151
Erickson, H. L., 108
Evergreen Point Bridge, 95

F

Faculty Center, 126, 127, *127*, 136
Father Neptune, 59, 111
Federal Urban Renewal funds, 144
Ferry, Elisha P., 18
Fine Arts Building, 68, 137. *See also* Architecture Hall
Firkins, Lyn, 7
Fisheries Center, 159
Fisheries Quadrangle, 166
Fisheries Teaching and Research Center, 166, *166*
Fisheries/Oceanography Library, 164
Fluke Hall, 127, *128*, 129
Fluke, John (family), 129

Foote, Donald J., 155
Forest Resources Library, 140
Forestry Building, 119
Fort Lawton, 18
Fountain of Reflection, 59, 79
Frasca, Robert, 50
Fred Bassetti & Company, 151
Frederick, D. E., 78
Freed, James Ingo, 50
French Renaissance, 72, 81
Friends of the Medicinal Herb Garden, 140
Frolich, Finn H., 56, 122, 151
Frosh Pond, *32, 33*, 44, *44*, 56, 134–135. *See also* Geyser Basin
Fuller, A. H., 22
Fuller Plan, *20*. *See also* Oval Plan

G

Gaines, Thomas A., 13
Gangnes, Arnold D., 159
Garfield Lane, 137
Garnett Schorr Architects, 60
Gatch, Thomas M., 18
Gates, Charles M., 11, 37–38
Gates, Mary, 134
Gates, William III, 134, 157
Geise, Jon, 108
George Washington Monument, 56, *56, 57*, 106
George Wellington Stoddard and Associates, 153
Gerberding Hall, 110–111, *112*. *See also* Administration Building
Gerberding, William P., 10–11, 13, 63, *63*, 66, 71
Getty, Lillian Brown, 38, 97
Geyser Basin, 29, 30, 135. *See also* Frosh Pond
GI Bill, 44, *44*, 47, *47*, 48
Giurgola, Romaldo, 60
Glenn Hughes Penthouse Theater, 75, 78
golf course, 43, 49, 157
Gould, Carl F., 10, 29, 30, *30*, 31–32, 34, 37, 38, 42, 44, 67, 79, 95, 97, 107, 108, 115, 118, 137, 146
Gould Hall, 133, 146, *147*
Gowen Hall, 38, *98–99*, 100, 145
Gowen, Herbert H., 100
Graduate Reading Room. *See* Suzzallo Reading Room
Grant, Copeland, Chervenak & Associates, 140
Grant Lane, 53, 108, 111
Graves Building, 154
Graves, Dorsett "Tubby", 154
Gregory, L. E., 157
Grieg Garden, 53, *54–55*, 56, 72, 73, 122
Grieg Statue, 56, 122, *123*
Guggenheim Hall, *58*, 59, 135
Guthrie Annex buildings, 141, *141*
Guthrie, Edwin R., 141
Guthrie Hall, 97, 141. *See also* Savery Hall

Gwathmey, Charles, 60
Gwathmey Siegel and Associates, 118
gymnasium, 21, 23, 84

H

Haggett, Arthur, 86
Haggett Hall, 86, 86, 87, 91
Haggett, Winifred S., 86
Hall, David C., 47, 124, 126
Hall Health Center, 46, 47
Halprin, Lawrence, 53
Hanna/Olin, Ltd., 122
Hansee Hall, 45, 85, 85
Hansee, Martha Lois, 85
Harmond, Prey & Dietrich, 122
Harris, Charles W., 162
Harris Hydraulics Laboratory, 162
Harvard University, 11
Hastings Group, The, 133
Hayden, James R., 18
Health Sciences Library and Information
    Center, 157
Heath, Gove & Bell/Lea, Pearson &
    Richards, 123
Henry Art Gallery, 115, 118, 118, 119
Henry, Horace C., 115, 118
Henry M. Jackson School of International
    Studies, 122
Hewitt Isley, 60
Hill, James J., 56, 151
Hindshaw, Henry H., 21, 44
Hitchcock, C. Leo, 159
Hitchcock Hall, 159
Home Economics Building. See Raitt Hall
Home Management House, 141
Hoo-Hoo House, 126, 127, 127
House Bill #470, 21
Howard & Galloway, 133, 145
HUB, 43, 48, 119, 120–121, 122
HUB Yard, 53, 73, 110, 119, 120–121
Hughes, Glenn A., 78
Husky Crew, 154, 155
Husky Stadium, 42, 150, 151, 153
Husky Union Building. See HUB
Hutchinson Hall, 43, 44, 91, 93
Hutchinson, Mary G., 93

I

Ibsen Nelsen & Associates, 166
Institute for Food Science and Technology,
    166
Interlaken, 18, 21, 23
International Grove, 119, 122
International Style, 126, 141, 159
Intramural Activities Building, 154
Inverarity, Robert B., 137

J

Jacob Lawrence Gallery, 103
Jacobsen, John T., 111
Jefferson Park, 18
Jensen, Ray, 108
John Graham and Associates, 85, 134, 135, 159
John M.Y. Lee & Partners, 110
John Morse/Clayton and Jean Young, 141
Johnson Hall, 44, 133
Johnson, Orson B., 133–134
Johnston, Norman J., 7, 7, 10, 11
Jones and Bindon, 122
Jones and Jones, 47, 129
Jones, John Paul, 122
Jones, Victor N., 111
Josenhans & Allan, 93, 123
Joyce, Copeland, Vaughan, & Nordfors, 122,
    146

K

Kallmann McKinnell and Wood Architects,
    79, 136
Kane Hall, 67, 103, 111, 113, 113, 116–117
Kane, Thomas F., 28–29, 111
Kellogg, David, 21
Kincaid Hall, 140
Kincaid, Trevor, 140–141
King Lane, 103
Kirk, Wallace, McKinley & Associates, 91,
    107, 115
Kirsten, Frederick K., 136
Kirsten Wind Tunnel, 135
Kirsten Wind Tunnel and Aeronautical
    Laboratory, 135–136
Kohn Pedersen Fox, 146
Kramer, Chin & Mayo, 155

L

Lake Union, 21, 141
Lake Washington, 21, 27, 129
Lake Washington Ship Canal, 38, 47, 129, 131,
    131
Lander, Edward, 146
Lander Hall, 146
landscaping, 21, 43, 43, 44, 53, 53, 60, 73, 101
Leary, Eliza Ferry, 78, 85
Leavenworth, Charles F., 18
Leiden University, 11
Leis, George, 155
Levine, Philip, 56, 144
Lewis, Alonzo Victor, 97
Lewis County, 15
Lewis Hall, 21, 69, 72, 91, 92, 93
Lewis, Meriwether, 91
Liberal Arts Quadrangle, 8–9, 29, 30, 38, 42,
    43, 48, 50, 51, 56, 67, 72, 95, 97, 98, 99,
    100, 149
libraries, 22, 29, 38, 39, 40–41, 42, 81, 107–110,
    119

Liddle & Jones, 162, 164
Loew, Edgar A., 151
Loew Hall, 151
logrolling, 32, 135
Loschky Marquardt and Nesholm, 60, 118,
    137
Lovelace, Arthur C., 145
Lundell, Gary, 7
Lyon Hall, 123

M

Machinery Hall, 151
MacKenzie, Donald H., 79
MacKenzie Hall, 50, 56, 79
Madrona Grove, 84
Magnuson Health Sciences Center, 47, 151,
    157, 159, 160–161
Magnuson, Warren G., 157
Mahlum and Nordfors, 136, 157
Mahlum & Nordfors McKinley Gordon, 146
Maki, Robert, 159
Mann, Fred, 7
Marine Sciences Building, 162, 164, 164
Marine Studies Building, 166, 166
Mary Gates Hall, 133, 134, 148. See also Physics
    Hall
Mathematics Research Library, 124
McCarty, Clara, 86
McCarty Hall, 86
McClelland & Jones, 157
McKee, Ruth Karr, 85
McKinley Architects, The, 154
McKinney, Michael, 60
McLeod Reckord, 166
McMahon, Edward, 91
McMahon Hall, 91, 91
McMahon, Theresa, 91
McReavey, John, 18
Meany, Edmond S., 10, 18, 20, 20, 21, 38, 43,
    44, 82, 101, 134, 137
Meany Hall, original, 42, 48, 66, 111, 115, 118,
    130
Meany Hall, present, 67, 107, 114, 115
Meany Hotel, 78
Mechanical Engineering Building, 151
Medicinal Herb Garden, 137, 137, 140
Memorial Gateway, 75
memorial pylons, 66, 75, 75
Memorial Way, 74, 75
Men's Athletic Pavilion, 153
Mercer, Asa Shinn, 16, 17, 149
Mercer Hall, 149
Metropolitan Tract, 10, 18, 19, 20, 21, 38, 63,
    66, 69, 136, 144, 146
Michael/Lakeman, 149
Microsoft, Inc., 108, 134, 157
Miller, Connie, 7
Miller Hall, 38, 96, 97, 98–99
Miller Hull Partnership, The, 155, 166
Miller, Pendleton, 129

Miller, William Winlock, 10, 97
Miss, Mary, 59, 159
MIT, 11
Mitchell/Giurgola Associates, 146
Mithun Partners, 149
modernism, 50, 86, 95
Montlake Bridge, 47, 131, 159, 167
Moore, Charles, 60
Moore, Ruble, Yudell, 137
More Hall, 151
Mount Rainier, 21, 23, 27
Mueller Hall, 152, 153
Mueller, James I., 153
Music Building, 101, 102, 103
Music Pavilion, 136
Mutai, Mituo, 79
Myers, David J., 85

N

Naramore, Granger & Thomas, 137
National Register, 69, 155
National Science Foundation, 137
Natural Sciences Library, 110
NBBJ, 47, 60, 129, 141, 153, 157, 166
Nelsen, Sabin & Varey, 145
Newman, Barnett, 56, 106
Nome Circle, 119
Nordstrom family, 154
Nordstrom Tennis Center, 153–154
Norling, Ernest, 122
North Campus, 75, 76 (map), 76–93
Northlake Urban Renewal Plan, 52–53, 59–60

O

Observatory, 21, 69, 76, 78, 93
Oceanography Building, 159, 160–161
Oceanography Teaching Building, 162
Odegaard, Charles E., 7, 10, 11, 47, 49, 49, 60, 95, 113
Odegaard Undergraduate Library, 67, 113, 115, 116–117
O'Higgins, Pablo, 113
Olin, Laurie, 50
Olmsted Brothers, 22, 29, 72, 134, 135, 166
Olmsted, John C., 22, 27
Olmsted 1904 Plan, 22, 22, 23
Olmsted 1914 Plan, 29, 30
Olympic Mountains, 21
One-Half Percent for Art fund, 59
Oregon State Pavilion, 119
Oval Plan, 22, 30. See also Fuller Plan

P

Padelford, Frederick M., 124
Padelford Hall, 124, 125
parking, 52, 84, 103, 153, 159, 166
Parrington Hall, 22, 24–25, 38, 69, 72, 82, 84, 93
Parrington, Vernon L., 38, 82–83

Paul Hayden Kirk & Associates, 79, 127
peacock window, 78
Pelli, Cesar, 60, 141
Pfeiffer, Norman, 50
Phi Mu, 79
Philosophy Hall. See Savery Hall
Physics/Astronomy Building, 12, 53, 63, 66, 67, 68, 75, 78, 95, 134, 141, 142–143, 144, 149
Physics Hall, 44, 133, 134, 141, 148. See also Mary Gates Hall
Physiology Hall, 130
Pi Beta Phi, 81
Piazza del Campo, 103
Pierrepont Hall, 91
Pike, John, 16
Playhouse, 145
Port Townsend, WA, 15
Portage Bay, 27, 47, 141, 160–161, 166
Post–World War II campus, 48, 48
Pratt, Dudley, 56, 100, 111, 118, 159
Princeton University, 11
Prohibition, 27
Provorse, Barry, 7
Public Arts Program, 59. See also One-Half Percent for Art fund
Public Works Administration, 66
Puget Sound, 21
Puget Sound Marine Station, 141

Q

Quaternary Research Building, 134

R

R. Bronsdon "Curly" Harris Alumni House, 84
Rainier Vista, 27, 43, 44, 60, 66, 72, 107, 113, 134, 135, 149
Raitt, Effie Isobel, 95
Raitt Hall, 35, 38, 72, 95, 97
Rand, Ted, 113
Red Square. See Central Plaza
Reed, Eleanor Henry, 144
Reed, William G. (family), 144
Regents Plan, 28, 30, 31, 31, 37, 38, 42, 43, 47, 48, 52, 66, 67, 72, 75, 82, 84, 101, 108, 118, 166
Revised General Plan of the University of Washington. See Regents Plan
Robert Billsbrough Price Associates, 154
Roberts Hall, 151, 152, 153
Roberts, Milnor, 151
Rockefeller Foundation, 159
Roethke Auditorium, 111
Roethke, Theodore, 111
Romanesque, 83
Royal A. McClure & Co., 149
Rupp, Christy, 59

S

Saarinen, Eero, 124
Sakuma, Donald, 166
Sakuma Viewpoint, 166
Salmon Homing Pond, 131, 159, 160–161
Sasaki, Hideo, 50
Saunders & Lawton, 133
Saunders, Charles W., 21, 78, 81, 82
Savery Hall, 38, 38, 97, 97
Savery, William, 97
Scandinavian Societies of the Northwest and Alaska, 122
Schmitz Hall, 56, 95, 144, 145
Schmitz, Henry, 144
Schwager, E. O., 21
Science Hall. See Parrington Hall
Science Quadrangle, 22, 30, 42, 43, 48, 133, 134, 136, 149
Seafirst Executive Education Center, 79
Seattle City Planning Commission, 50, 52
Seattle Park Plan, 22
Seattle Repertory Theater, 145
Seattle, WA, 15, 16 (map), 17, 17
Seattle World's Fair, 50, 79
Shell House, original, 154, 154
Shellhouse Annex, 154
Shinbo, Robert, 122
Shipscalers, Drydock, and Boatworkers Union, 113
Shipscalers' Mural, 113
Sieg Hall, 50, 50, 95, 122
Sieg, Lee Paul, 122
Skagit Lane, 100
Skilling Ward Magnusson Barkshire, Inc., 153
Smith, Charles W., 108
Smith Hall, 38, 98–99, 100–101
Smith, James Allen, 100
Smith Room, 36, 37
Smith Wing, 6, 7, 108, 109
Social Science Hall. See Smith Hall
South Campus, 75, 151, 152 (map), 152–167
South Campus Center, 159, 160–161, 162, 164
Southwest Campus Plan, 71, 141, 149, 164, 166
Sproule, John R., 141
Stanford University, 11
Steinbrueck, Victor, 127
Stetho, 159
Stevens Court, 149
Stevens, Isaac I., 149
Stevens Way, 44, 91, 122, 140
Streeter Dermanis, 166
Streissguth, Dan, 146
Student Union Building, 43, 48, 56, 123. See also HUB
Sturtevant, Butler S., 44
Sullivan, Woodruff, 141
sundial, 1912, 13, 83
sundial, Physics/Astronomy Building, 73, 141
Suzzallo, Henry, 10, 31, 34, 37, 37, 38, 42, 48, 49, 67, 97, 107, 111, 115, 118, 157

Suzzallo Library, *6, 7, 36, 37, 38, 39, 40–41,* 50, 56, 60, *61,* 66, *94, 95,* 107, *107, 113,* 119
Suzzallo Reading Room, *94, 95,* 107, 108
SWA, 153
Sylvan Theater, *69, 69, 72,* 136

T

Taft, Larado, 56, 106
Territorial University of Washington, 16, 17, *17, 18, 18*
Terry, Charles C., 15, 146
Terry Hall, 146
Terry, Mary, 15
Terry, Roland, 84
The First Century at the University of Washington, 10
The Waiting Multitude, 108
Thiry, Paul, 50, 52, 53, 66, 136
Thomas G. Thompson, the *164, 165*
Thomson, David, 122
Thomson Hall, 122
Tobey, Mark, 145
TRA, 60, 157, 159
Trask, Tallman III, 11, 63
Triangle Parking Garage, 66, 153
Tsutakawa, George, 56, *59, 79*
Tucker & Shields, 122
Turnball, Francis J., 103

U

Union Bay Place, 48
Union Street, 17
University Bridge, 42. *See also* Campus Parkway
University Commercial Club, 42
University Flagpole, 83
University Land and Building Commission, 18, 20, 21
University Land Commission, 15
University of California, 11
University of Cambridge, 11, 34
University of Heidelberg, 11
University of Illinois, 11
University of Michigan, 11
University of North Carolina, 11
University of Oregon Medical School, 157
University of Oslo, 11
University of Oxford, 11, 34
University of Paris–Sorbonne, 11
University of Washington, 7, 10–11, 13
  Alumni Association, 66, 84, 113
  Architectural Commission, 50
  Board of Regents, 17, 21, 22, 28–29, 30, 42, 79, 85, 107, 111, 113, 134
    Building and Grounds Committee, 42, 97
  campus, 1914, 30–31, *30–31;* 1920 plan, *38, 38;* 1935 plan, 47, 48; 1948 plan, 48–49, 52; 1949 plan, 48, *48*

Campus Planning Office, 53
General Development Plan, 50, 52
General Physical Development Plan, 71, 101
Landscape Advisory Committee, 53
Language Learning Center, 81
Libraries, Special Collections and Preservation, 110
Master Plan, 71
Medical Center, 47, 157, *158,* 159, *160–161*
University of Washington,
  College of Architecture and Urban Planning, 130, 146
  College of Arts and Sciences, 50, 123, 124
  College of Education, 97
  College of Engineering, 97, 151
  College of Forest Resources, 129, 140
  Department of Aeronautics and Astronautics, 135
  Department of Anthropology, 81
  Department of Asian Languages and Literature, 100
  Department of Astronomy, 134
  Department of Building Construction, 133
  Department of Chemical Engineering, 137
  Department of Chemistry, 137
  Department of Civil Engineering, 151
  Department of Classics, 81
  Department of Computer Science and Engineering, 122
  Department of Economics, 97
  Department of Geography, 100
  Department of Germanics, 81
  Department of History, 100
  Department of Materials Science and Engineering, 151
  Department of Near Eastern Languages and Literature, 81
  Department of Physics, 134
  Department of Political Science, 100
  Department of Psychology, 141
  Department of Sociology, 97
  Department of Speech Communication, 95
  Department of Zoology, 140
  School of Art, 101
  School of Business Administration, 79
  School of Communications, 93, 123
  School of Dentistry, 47
  School of Drama, 93
  School of Fisheries, 159
  School of Home Economics, 95
  School of Law, 47, 100, 145–146
  School of Marine Affairs, 166
  School of Medicine, 47, *49,* 157
  School of Music, 101
  School of Nursing, 47, *162*
  School of Oceanography, 159, 164
  School of Pharmacy, 137
University of Wisconsin, 11
University Village Shopping Center, 48

University Way NE, "the Ave," 84
U.S. Government Building, 103, 135
U.S. News & World Report, 63

V

Vancouver, WA, 15
Varey, Gordon B., 4
Vietnam War, 103
Virginia Wright Foundation, 106

W

Waldron & Pomeroy, 144
Waldron Pomeroy Smith Foote and Akira, 157
Walker Ames Room, 111
Walker and McGough, 52, 53, 66, 107, 124
Walker, McGough, Foltz, Lyerla, 113
Walker, Peter, 50
Walla Walla, WA, 15
Washington elm, the, 123
Washington State Legislature, 18, 27, 63, 95, 97, 106–107, 157
Washington State Pavilion, 76, 107, 119
Washington State Register of Historic Places, 69, 81, 82
Washington State University / King County Cooperative Extension, 129
Washington Technology Center. *See* Fluke Hall
Washington, Territorial Legislature of, 15, 16, 17
Waterfront Activities Center, 155
Webster, John, 15
Weibell, Gottlieb, 81
Weiss, Dick, 166
Whitehouse & Price, 103
Winkenwerder Hall, 140
Winkenwerder, Hugo, 140
Women's Building, 133, *133*
World War I, 38, 75, *75,* 76, 97
World War II, 44, 50, 85, 100, 111, 126, 137, 157
Wurster, William, 50

X Y

Yale University, 11
Yamasaki, Minoru, 50
YMCA, 22
Yomiuri Shimbun, 79
Yoshino cherry trees. *See* cherry trees
Young and Richardson, 159
Young, Richardson and Carleton, 86, 136
Young, Richardson, Carleton and Detlie, 146

Z

Zema, Gene, 146
Zentz, Patrick, 159